Understanding Intellectual Property Rights

Module 1: Introduction

Lesson 1: Introduction to IP Protection

Intellectual Property Protection: An Example of What Is at Stake for Small Business

In the early 2000s, Commerce Electronics Corp. (CEC) noticed that its European sales had begun dropping for no apparent reason. CEC, a small maker of control panels for high-end kitchen appliances, was perplexed because Europe had always been a predictable source of revenue. Soon, CEC discovered that a Chinese company was counterfeiting its products, going so far as to print CEC's name, address, and catalog number on the fake control panels. As a result of the counterfeiting, CEC estimates that it has lost approximately 10 to 12 jobs so far and $1 million in annual revenue, a lot for a small company.

Companies like CEC have a lot to lose from infringement of intellectual property rights (IPRs). They suffer lost sales, they pay to replace the defective fake counterfeits, they may be sued for personal injury from the defective counterfeit products, and perhaps most damaging of all, the goodwill and reputation of the company, often developed over many years, are eroded.

This course is designed to help small businesses take steps to protect themselves against the type of losses that CEC and many others have suffered as a result of IPR infringement within the United States and abroad. Although this course is designed for small businesses, the information presented is useful for all businesses, large or small.

Introduction to IPRs

Success in today's global economy is increasingly dependent upon effective identification, protection, and enforcement of intellectual property (IP) assets. In fact, IP-based businesses and entrepreneurs today drive more economic growth in the United States than any other single sector. According to the 2006 Economic Report of the President:

- IP accounts for approximately 1/3 of the value of U.S. corporations
- U.S. IP may be worth more than $5 trillion

In 2003, IP and IP support industries represented over 17 percent of the U.S. gross domestic product.

Many small businesses are only now becoming aware of the nature and extent of their assets and the extent to which those assets may be protected by one or more types of IPRs.

Unfortunately, as technology advances have made the large-scale copying and distribution of pirated and counterfeit goods easy and inexpensive, theft of IP has become increasingly widespread. Today, piracy, counterfeiting, and other theft of IP assets pose a serious threat to all U.S. businesses.

Given the significant threat of IP theft to both the success of individual companies and the economy as a whole, protection of IP assets is critical whether you are a major multinational firm or a single-person, home-based business. While some smaller businesses may be quick to dismiss the protection of IP assets as "something only bigger companies can do," the failure to identify, protect, and enforce IPRs can mean the difference between a business's continued existence as a company and its closing.

Defining IPRs

IPRs are rights that pertain to creations of the human mind. Individuals, corporations, or other entities may claim them. IPRs typically give the owner of the IP the exclusive right to control use of the creation for a certain period of time. Laws governing IPRs are intended to stimulate innovation and creativity, ensure fair competition, and protect consumers.

IPRs include the following:

- Copyrights and related rights
- Trademarks (including geographical indications)
- Patents
- Industrial designs, integrated circuit designs and plant varieties
- Trade secrets

Importance of IP Protection to Small Business

Recent reports, such as those showing that small businesses now produce 13 to 14 times more patents per employee than large companies, demonstrate the critical role that small businesses play in innovation and the success of the U.S. economy. Protecting the IP associated with their innovations is critical to small businesses on a number of levels. IP can enable a small business to:

- Reap profits from its ideas and creations and from licensing its rights
- Preserve a market niche and thereby compete effectively with larger companies
- Establish and grow its reputation and goodwill in the marketplace

IP can also:

- Enhance the worth of a small business in the eyes of investors and financing institutions
- Raise the value of a small business in the event of a sale or merger

Example of How IP Protection Can Help a Small Business Succeed

In 2001, Solartex, Inc. (Solartex), a small solar energy research and development company, invented a fabric that absorbs solar energy and converts it into thermal energy. Winter clothing made from the fabric is both extremely lightweight and very warm even in the coldest temperatures.

Prior to disclosing its invention to the public, Solartex applied for and was granted patents for its revolutionary fabric in the United States and overseas. Solartex adopted the brand name "Suntex" for its fabric after a thorough search of trademarks in use throughout the world. It immediately filed applications to register the Suntex trademark and an associated logo in the United States and throughout Europe, Asia, and Central and South America.

After its launch, Suntex fabric was an immediate worldwide sensation. Because Solartex had obtained patents for the fabric at home and abroad, it was secure in its position as exclusive manufacturer and supplier of solar energy fabric. The company quickly grew and expanded. Solartex's trademark registrations for the Suntex name and logo in the United States and overseas allowed Solartex to effectively protect and control the Suntex brand and image as the company's sales increased.

In 2006, Solartex was sold for $500 million. The company's high valuation was based primarily upon sales of Suntex fabric and the IPRs associated with that product. If Solartex had not taken steps to carefully protect its IPRs in Suntex at the outset, the fate of the company would likely have been very different.

Vulnerability of Small Business to IP Theft

Protecting valuable IP assets is particularly critical for small business owners, and it is also particularly challenging. Effective protection of IP can be difficult for small businesses because they often lack:

- Experience in protecting IP, which may result in small businesses entering markets without taking adequate precautions against IP theft
- In-house legal expertise (or even an outside attorney, especially one with IP expertise)
- Financial resources to engage in protracted IP litigation or to undertake large-scale anticounterfeiting and antipiracy operations

In addition to lacking the resources and expertise of larger companies, small businesses are also particularly vulnerable to IP theft because they often do not have other product lines to fall back on in the event that an IP asset is stolen.

Module 2: IP Protection and Your Business

Lesson 1: Does Your Business Need IP Protection?

Introduction

If you are a new business, or if you have been in business but have not yet taken steps to protect your intellectual property rights (IPRs) at home and abroad, you may be unsure what IP rights your business has to protect. If you feel you do not have an adequate understanding of your business's IPRs, you are not alone. For example, a study performed by the U.S. Patent and Trademark Office shows that 85% of businesses do not understand that U.S. patent and trademark registrations do not provide intellectual property (IP) protection in overseas markets.

Next, there is a questionnaire that will enable you to assess the nature of your business's IPRs.

Needs Assessment: Does Your Business Own IP?

To determine the types of IPRs you may need to protect:

- Read the following 15 questions listed below.
- As you go through the assessment, write down your response to each question (i.e., "yes" or "no").
- Instructions for analyzing the assessment results are provided at the end of the assessment.

Needs Assessment Questions

1. Does your business have a name or logo by which it represents itself to customers (e.g., "Nike" or "Delta Airlines")?

2. Does your business design or create any computer hardware or software?

3. Does your business have any confidential information that gives it an advantage over its competitors (e.g., product formulas, manufacturing processes, customer lists, marketing strategies, computer source code, pricing information, financial data, supplier lists)?

4. Does your business use any brand names or logos in connection with specific products it sells or services it offers (e.g., Nike's "Airwalk" line of shoes or Delta Airlines' "SkyMiles" program)?

5. Does your business design or create any machines, tools, instruments, methods, systems, processes, compounds, formulations or medicines?

6. Does your business sell any products that have unique colors, smells or sounds that distinguish those products from those of your competitors?

7. Does your business create, or participate in the creation of, any original art, graphic design, photography, written articles, poetry, books, music, films or dramatic works?

8. Does your business participate in the production, performance, or broadcast of sound recordings, radio and television broadcasts, or live artistic performances?

9. Does your business sell a product in packaging that has a unique shape or design?

10. Does your business create, or participate in the creation of, architectural drawings?

11. Does your business use any advertising slogans to sell its services or products?

12. Does your business use catalogs, brochures, flyers, or manuals?

13. Does your business design or create any useful products that have a unique shape or design?

14. Does your business create, or participate in the creation of, textile, apparel or accessory designs?

15. Does your business have a Web site or does it market or sell any products via the Internet?

Analyzing the Assessment Results

- If you answered yes to questions 1, 4, 6, 9, or 11, then your business likely has trademark rights that require protection.
- If you answered yes to questions 2, 7, 8, 10, 12, 14, or 15, then your business likely has copyright rights that require protection.
- If you answered yes to question 3, then your business likely has trade secret rights that require protection.
- If you answered yes to questions 5, 13, or 14, than your business likely has patent rights that require protection.

Information about these rights, and steps you can take to protect and enforce them in the Unites States and abroad, is presented in the remaining lessons of this course.

Conducting an IP Audit

Before you can take effective steps to protect the IPRs of your business, you must have a complete understanding of the nature and value of your IP. The best way to achieve this understanding is to conduct an IP audit of your business.

An IP audit is a systematic review of the IP owned, used, or acquired by a business. The goals of an IP audit are to:

- Identify all the IP owned or used by the business
- Consider appropriate ways to protect the IP owned by the business
- Provide the information necessary to value these intangible business assets

As a small business owner, you may conduct an informal IP audit using publicly-available information (see examples of sources in the Resource Center). Consider using the advice and input of an IP attorney to help you develop your IP strategy. A financial advisor also can help you determine the commercial value of any particular IP asset that may influence your IP strategy.

Importance of an IP Audit

An IP audit provides numerous important benefits for a business. For example, it:

- Forces a business to think about and identify the IP assets it owns and the strategies that may be used to protect each asset
- Forces a business to consider the extent to which it relies on others' IP, evaluate its licenses, and explore the need to develop its own IP
- Provides the information necessary to ensure that adequate steps are being taken to protect all IP assets
- Provides the information necessary to value IP assets that may be an important component of the business's overall valuation
- Can help a business increase its cash flow by licensing IPRs to a third party
- Can help a business identify possible assets that could be used as collateral for financing
- Supports cost-benefit analysis of enforcement decisions
- Reduces costs by eliminating costs associated with obsolete IP
- Assists in ensuring proper use of others' IP
- Assists in ensuring proper use of the business's own IP
- Assists in determining how tax payments should be made (some countries allow property taxes to be amortized over the life of the asset)

Mechanics of an IP Audit

An IP audit should cover the business assets that are owned, licensed, or incorporated into a business's products and services. For assets that a company owns, the company should determine:

- The type(s) of IP protection that may be available to protect each of the business's assets
- The countries, regions, or markets where each IP asset needs protection (including the need to protect IP assets against IP theft in connection with the company's website)
- Whether, and to what extent, the type(s) of IP protection identified are available in a particular country
- The duration, or "life," of each type of IP
- The costs of protecting the IP asset in a particular country (and, conversely, the potential costs of failing to protect the IP asset in that country)
- The value of each IP asset to the company and whether it merits protection in a particular country. The value of an IP asset can be determined by:

  o The contribution the asset makes to the business
  o Its resale and license value
  o The amount invested to develop it
  o The amount the business would be willing to invest to protect or enforce against infringement

An IP audit also enables you to ensure that any use by your business of others' IP assets is properly licensed or otherwise authorized by the third party (preferably in writing). Some uses of third-party materials may fall within the "fair use" provisions of trademark and copyright law. Most commercial uses of third-party materials, however, will not.

An example of a company's IP audit can be viewed at the following website:
http://www.wipo.int/sme/en/documents/ip_audit.htm

Every business, regardless of size, should conduct an initial IP audit to determine what assets the business owns, whether and to what extent the asset can be protected through IPRs, and in which country or countries the business should consider seeking protection. The frequency with which a company should conduct an IP audit depends upon the size and nature of the business. However, an IP audit should always be conducted in connection with certain events, such as the establishment of a Web site, the purchase or sale of the business, the licensing of IPRs to third parties, or the expansion of the business to new countries, regions, or markets.

Module 3: Understanding Different Types of IPRs

Lesson 1: Introduction

Introduction

The term "intellectual property" encompasses a variety of rights that can be claimed by individuals or entities. These rights include the following:

- Copyright and related rights
- Trademarks (including geographical indications)
- Patents
- Industrial designs and integrated circuit designs
- Trade secrets

Lesson 2: Copyright

Introduction to Copyright

The area of copyright confronts some of the most widely publicized intellectual property (IP) issues today--software piracy, music file sharing, film and video game piracy. Technological advances such as digitization and the Internet have made reproduction and global distribution of copyrighted works both easy and inexpensive. As a result, copyright enforcement has become an issue of primary concern for businesses around the world.

Every business has materials, such as marketing materials, that are protected by copyright. In addition, your business will want to avoid infringing the copyright rights of others.

Definition of Copyright

Copyright is a form of legal protection granted to the authors of original creative works. Copyright is used to protect a wide range of subject matter, including:

- Literary works
- Musical works
- Dramatic works
- Pantomimes and choreographic works
- Architectural works
- Pictorial, graphic, and sculptural works
- Motion pictures and other audiovisual works
- Sound recordings

- Computer programs

Contrary to popular belief, copyright protection extends only to the tangible expression of an idea, not to the idea itself.

Common Business Materials Protected by Copyright

Virtually every business, large or small, creates materials that are protected by copyright. Common examples include:

- Brochures
- Catalogs
- Advertising
- Instruction manuals
- Logos
- Web sites

Rights Afforded by Copyright

Simply stated, the copyright owner has the **exclusive** right to do and to authorize others to do any of the following:

- Copy the work
- Change the work
- Distribute the work publicly
- Perform or display the work publicly.

The following is an example of a hypothetical copyright owner and the various ways in which she can control and exploit her copyrighted work:

Annie Gesso is a young painter whose works have caused a worldwide sensation. One of her paintings was printed on the cover of Time magazine, with her permission. Annie owns the copyright in all of her paintings.

Since her work appeared on the cover of Time, Annie has been inundated with requests to use her paintings in various ways, including:

- Displaying the paintings in modern art museums
- Printing and selling posters of the paintings
- Reproducing images of the paintings on note cards and calendars
- Using her paintings on the set of a new movie
- Creating a children's book with illustrations based on modified versions of her paintings

It is within Annie's rights as a copyright owner to authorize and control all of these uses of her work.

Creation of a Copyright

In the United States and in most other countries, copyright protection does not depend upon any official procedures or formalities. Rather, a creative work is considered protected by copyright as soon as it exists, so long as it is both **original** and **fixed in a tangible form**.

Originality

In copyright law, "originality" means that the work was independently created by the author and has some minimal degree of creativity. "Independently created" simply means that the work must be the independent product of the author and not copied from someone else's work. A work can be original without being novel or unique.
For example, an author's new book "How to Pick Stocks and Get Rich," is original in the copyright sense so long as the author did not create the book by copying existing material, even if it is the millionth book written on the subject of choosing stocks.

Fixed in a Tangible Form

"Fixed in a tangible form" means that the work is sufficiently permanent or stable to permit it to be perceived, reproduced, or otherwise communicated for a period of more than transitory duration. It makes no difference what the form, manner, or medium of expression is. Words, for example, can be fixed by writing them down, typing them on an old-fashioned typewriter, dictating them into a tape recorder, or entering them into a computer.

A copyright concept related to the requirement of fixation is that of idea versus expression. Specifically, copyright does not protect mere ideas; it protects the manner in which an artist expresses an idea, whether in words, painting, sculpture, or any other tangible form. Copyright protects against others simply copying an artist's work, but it does not prevent other artists from creating their own original expressions of the same idea.

For example:

- Anyone can use the idea of a hero with superhuman powers. However, only the copyright owners of "Superman" can publish stories about that particular superhero and the world they have developed around that character.
- Anyone can use the idea of a boy who discovers he has magical powers. However, only J.K. Rowling can publish stories about Harry Potter or any of the other characters who populate her books.

Although registration is not required to protect a copyright, many countries do have registration systems. In many of these countries, registration makes it easier for copyright owners to prove copyright infringement cases in court. In the United States, owners of works of U.S. origin must register their copyright in order to initiate a case in U.S. court. Copyright registration:

- Reflects the date on which the author established ownership with the Library of Congress.
- Is generally necessary for border enforcement of copyrights.

In addition, although a copyright registration is not required in the United States, the U.S. Copyright Act establishes a mandatory deposit requirement for works published in the United States. For more information on this requirement, go to: http://www.copyright.gov/circs/circ07d.html.

Duration of a Copyright

In the United States, the length of time a copyright is protected (for works originally created on or after January 1, 1978) is:

- The life of the author plus 70 years, if the owner is a person
- 95 years from publication or 120 years from creation of the work, whichever is shorter, if the owner is a corporation or other entity

For works created prior to 1978, duration is governed by the copyright act of 1909, which provided an initial 28 year term of protection with possibility of subsequent renewal.

In other countries, the term of protection for a copyright varies. WTO members are obligated to provide a minimum term of protection of life of the author plus 50 years. Increasingly, countries are establishing longer terms of copyright protection. For example, the European Commission, like the United States, has extended the term of protection to 70 years after the author's death. Mexico affords the longest term of protection--the life of the author plus 100 years.

Ownership of a Copyright

As a general rule, the person who created a work is considered its author and the owner of the copyright in the work. However, there are exceptions to this rule, the most significant of which are:

- Work Made for Hire

    Under the "work made for hire" doctrine, if an employee creates a work in the course of his or her employment, the employer--not the employee--is considered the author of the work and the owner of the copyright in it. This is the law in the United States and some countries in Europe. In other countries, the employee owns the copyright unless there is a specific contract transferring the copyright to the employer.

For example, ABC Software, Inc. (ABC), a U.S. company, assigns Tim Smith, one of its junior programmers, to work on a program to assist real estate investors with managing their investment properties. Tim develops the software product virtually on his own, with no assistance from others in the company. Once completed, the product is an unexpected success, and the company realizes tens of millions of dollars in revenue from it. Nonetheless, Tim's only reward for his work, in addition to his regular salary, is a $500 end-of-year bonus. Tim is bitter and sues ABC, claiming the copyright in the software is owned by him because he created it. Tim will lose this case because he created the software as an employee of ABC, and the creation of the software was within the scope of his duties as a programmer for the company. As such, the copyright in the software is automatically owned by ABC.

If Tim had been working as an independent contractor, the results of his lawsuit may have been quite different. In that case, Tim would have owned the copyright in the software unless he signed an agreement transferring ownership of the copyright to ABC. The results of Tim's lawsuit might also have been different if Tim had been employed as an accountant, rather than as a computer programmer, for ABC. In that case, the creation of a computer program likely would have been considered outside the scope of Tim's employment, and Tim may have won the case.

Note that this hypothetical example reflects the law in the United States and some other countries. In certain other countries, the law with regard to employer/employee creations is exactly the opposite.

- Joint Work

A "joint work" is created when two or more authors agree that their contributions to a particular work are to be merged together to form an integrated or interdependent whole. If a joint work has been formed, each contributor is considered the author of the entire work, and all contributors are deemed to be co-owners of the copyright in the entire work unless they agree otherwise (preferably in writing). For example, a band that creates a song together through contributions by all band members would be considered a joint work.

- Contracts that transfer copyright ownership

Note that ownership of an item, such as a CD or book, is not the same as owning the copyright in the item. The owner of the item may sell, lend, or give it away, but he or she may not make additional copies or do anything else that the copyright owner has the exclusive right to do.

Businesses should clarify in their contracts who owns the IP and what types of work are covered by the contract. Businesses are often surprised to learn that outside graphics and Web site designers own the copyrights in the commissioned works in the absence of a written transfer of the copyright.

Using Third-Party Material

It is important to remember that all of the rights that exist in your business's marketing brochures, Web site and other materials also exist in the materials of third parties. In the course of your business's activities, you must be careful to ensure that you do not unknowingly violate someone else's copyright.

Today, the most common source of unintentional copyright infringement is the Internet. There is a common misperception that any material posted on the Internet is free for others to use and copy. To the contrary, copying any material from a third-party Web site, including text, photos, graphics, or other elements of another's Web site content, is unlawful. For example, if a company needs an image of an elephant to include on a clever marketing piece it is sending out, it cannot simply find an elephant image on National Geographic's Web site and copy it. The most likely lawful source of such an image would be a stock photo Web site, from which an elephant image could be selected and the right to use that image purchased.

Note, however, that if the copyright in the published material has expired, it may be considered to have fallen into the public domain and would, therefore, be free for anyone to use.

Lesson 3: Trademarks

Introduction to Trademarks

A company's trademarks are often its most important assets. Nike's "Swoosh," McDonald's "Golden Arches," the names Coca-Cola, Starbucks and Amazon.com--all of these marks immediately conjure up certain feelings and images in the minds of consumers that these companies have worked extremely hard to achieve. The worldwide nature of the Internet and the increasing globalization of business-- through something as simple as having a Web site--have made protection and enforcement of these assets both more important and more difficult.

Definition of Trademark

A trademark is a word, phrase, symbol or design-- or a combination of any of these--that serves to identify and distinguish a specific product or service from others in the marketplace.

The term "service mark" rather than "trademark" is sometimes used when referring to a mark used in connection with a service rather than a product. For example, the mark H&R BLOCK would be a service mark because it is used in connection with a service-- income tax preparation. However, in common usage, the term "trademark" is applied to marks for both goods and services.

In some instances, the following things can serve as trademarks as well:

- Colors

  Many countries accept color combination marks for registration, but they may condition registration upon proof that the color combination has become distinctive as a trademark through use. International law leaves open the question of whether a single color may be protected as a trademark. At present, there is significant disagreement among nations on this issue. In the United States, single color marks may be protected only if they can be shown to have acquired distinctiveness as trademarks (e.g., UPS's use of the color brown for package delivery services). In China and Japan, single color marks are not registrable under any circumstances. In addition, colors that are functional (i.e., essential to the use or purpose of the product or that affect the cost or quality of the product) are not protectable.

- Smells

  International law does not require that scent marks be protected as trademarks. In the United States, scents have in some circumstances been found to be protectable as trademarks (e.g., a floral scent for sewing thread).

- Sounds

  As is the case with scent marks, international law does not require countries to protect sound marks. The United States, however, has long recognized sound marks as protectable trademarks, such as the well-known NBC chimes or the famous roar of the MGM lion.

- Product Shapes

  Most countries, including the United States, permit the protection of product shapes as trademarks under certain circumstances. One of the most well-known examples is the distinctive shape of the Coca-Cola bottle. Protection of product shape is generally limited to cases in which the shape is nonfunctional and where it has acquired distinctiveness through use. Product packaging, on the other hand, may be inherently distinctive.

  A product's shape or design, packaging, color, or other distinguishing nonfunctional element of appearance is generally referred to as "trade dress."

Some examples of well known trademarks include:

- REGAL CINEMAS for cinemas
- BEN & JERRY'S for ice cream
- Apple Computer's "Apple" logo for computers
- Timex's slogan "It takes a licking and keeps on ticking" for watches

– FAHRVERGNUGEN for Volkswagen cars

Scope of Marks Eligible for Protection

Not all trademarks are created equal. There are significant differences in the types of marks that can function as trademarks and the extent to which they may be eligible for protection in any given country. Understanding these differences is essential to choosing a new trademark that can be protected in all relevant markets. It is also important to understand that there are some categories of terms that for public policy reasons can never be used as trademarks. Most countries exclude some categories of terms and symbols from trademark protection entirely. In addition to generic terms, excluded marks include:

– Marks used for official government business (e.g., national flags, coats of arms, national emblems, etc.)
– Marks that are deceptive regarding the nature or origin of the products or services to which they apply (e.g., the mark FRESH-PICKED JUICE for a beverage containing no real fruit juice or the mark GLASS WAX for a window cleaning product containing no wax)
– Marks that are considered to be against public order, morally offensive, or obscene

In general, a trademark will receive protection if it is arbitrary or fanciful, or suggestive, but not if the term is merely descriptive of the product or service it represents. Here are some examples of highly distinctive marks:
– KODAK
– APPLE
– GOOGLE
– EXXON
– BLUETOOTH

Types of Marks

The types of marks that can be protected as trademarks fall upon a continuum, with fanciful, arbitrary, and suggestive marks being the most protectable and descriptive and generic marks being the least protectable (generic marks are never protectable under any circumstances). The following table illustrates the various types of marks and the extent to which they are protectable as trademarks:

Strength of Mark	Type of Mark	Examples	Protection Available
Strongest	Coined or fanciful (invented terms)	KODAK, VERIZON, STARBUCKS, EXXON, REEBOK	Provided that they are not confusingly similar to third-party marks for similar goods and services, fanciful marks are protectable in all countries.

Strength of Mark	Type of Mark	Examples	Protection Available
Strong	Arbitrary (common words that have no relationship to the product or service)	APPLE for computers, AMAZON.COM for Internet retail services, DIESEL for clothing, BLUETOOTH for wireless interconnectivity products	Provided that others in the same field are not using the same or similar marks, arbitrary marks generally are protectable in all countries.
Fairly Strong	Suggestive (marks that hint at, or indirectly allude to, a quality or feature of the product or service)	CHICKEN OF THE SEA for tuna fish, PLAYSKOOL for toys, COPPERTONE for suntan lotion	Suggestive marks are protectable as trademarks, but they are not as strong as fanciful and arbitrary marks and there is a risk that countries may reach different conclusions as to whether a mark is suggestive or is unprotectable as a merely descriptive term. (Example: DOUBLEMINT was considered suggestive for chewing gum by the U.S. Patent and Trademark Office, but the United Kingdom deemed it to be merely descriptive and hence unprotectable.)
Weak (but can become distinctive)	Descriptive (terms that describe some characteristic or quality of the product or service)	YELLOW PAGES for telephone listings printed on yellow paper, PARK 'N FLY for airport parking lots	Descriptive terms are not protectable as trademarks. However, descriptive marks may become protectable over time by gaining secondary meaning through extensive and exclusive use. In the examples provided, YELLOW PAGES is a merely descriptive term and cannot be registered in the United States.
Weak (but can become strong)	Personal Names	KEN'S for salad dressing, HOWARD JOHNSON'S for hotels, DELL for computers	In the United States, surnames and "family" names are generally treated like descriptive terms.
None	Generic (the common word	MILK for milk, COMPUTER for	Generic terms may not be protected under any

Strength of Mark	Type of Mark	Examples	Protection Available
	for a product or service)	computers, APPLE for apples	circumstances.

Territoriality of Trademarks

Trademark rights are territorial, meaning that protection in one country does not mean that protection exists in any other country. Each country has its own specific requirements, such as use and/or registration, that must be met in order to obtain trademark protection in that country. A U.S. trademark registration, for example, protects a trademark only in the United States.

The territorial nature of trademark protection is very different from copyright protection, which does not depend upon procedures or formalities in individual countries. The mere creation of a copyrightable work is generally sufficient for copyright protection to exist in most countries of the world. Although it is often beneficial to register the copyright, it is not necessary to do so for copyright protection to exist.) With regard to trademarks, however, each country has its own procedures or formalities that must be followed for trademark protection to exist. One exception to this general principle is that famous marks may receive trademark protection even when they have not been used or registered in a particular country.

First to Use vs. First to File

Anyone seeking to protect trademarks in other countries must first understand that countries fall into two basic categories with respect to establishing trademark rights:

- **First to Use:** In the United States, Canada, the U.K., and some other countries, trademark ownership is established by *use of the mark in connection with goods or services*. In these "first to use" countries, rights exist upon use in commerce, although a registration provides important benefits to the trademark owner.
- **First to File:** In most other countries, trademark rights are established only through *registration*. In these "first to file" countries, the first party to register a mark with the local trademark office is considered the owner regardless of whether someone else used the mark in that country first. Therefore, your business may want to consider filing for trademark protection prior to introducing a new product.

Duration of Trademarks

If properly maintained, trademark rights can last forever. In the United States, rights in a trademark depend upon continued use of the mark. (Registration is not required but does confer significant benefits.) If a mark falls out of use for a sufficient length of time, others may be able to use the mark. If the mark is registered, others can petition to cancel the registration because of failure to use the mark. Because trademark rights in the United States depend upon use, not registration, a trademark owner's failure to renew a U.S. registration does not necessarily mean that rights in the mark have been abandoned.

In "first to file" countries, continued rights in a trademark depend upon timely renewal of the trademark registration. A trademark registration, once obtained, is valid for a specific length of time (which varies by country), but the registration can be renewed indefinitely if proper procedures are followed. In most countries, trademark registrations are valid for a term of 10 years, after which they must be renewed.

Collective Membership Marks and Certification Marks

The purpose of an ordinary trademark or service mark is to identify to consumers the actual source—the maker or provider—of the goods or services with which the mark is used. There are two special types of marks, however, in which the registrants of the marks are not the users of them. They are:

- Collective Marks

  There are two types of collective marks in the United States:

  o Collective trademarks (or collective service marks). A collective trademark or collective service mark is a mark adopted by a "collective" (i.e., an association, union, cooperative, fraternal organization, or other organized collective group) for use only by its members, who in turn use the mark to identify their goods or services and distinguish them from those of non-members. The "collective" itself neither sells goods nor performs services under a collective trademark or collective service mark, but the collective may advertise or otherwise promote the goods or services sold or rendered by its members under the mark.

  o Collective membership marks. A collective membership mark is a mark adopted for the purpose of indicating membership in an organized collective group, such as a union, an association, or other organization. Neither the collective nor its members uses the collective membership mark to identify and distinguish goods or services; rather, the sole function of such a mark is to indicate that the person displaying the mark is a member of the organized collective group.

  Examples of collective marks in the United States include the American Automobile Association (AAA) and Florists Transworld Delivery (FTD).

- Certification Marks

  A certification mark is used to identify goods or services that meet certain criteria such as quality, origin, material, or other characteristics. Typically, a system of rating is established by an independent organization, and the symbol is then licensed to approved manufacturers or service providers. Examples of certification marks include the Good Housekeeping Seal of Approval (which certifies that a product meets a certain level of quality and reliability), Underwriters Laboratories' UL mark (which certifies compliance with UL's safety requirements), and the Woolmark symbol (which certifies that certain laundry products can wash and dry wool and wool-blend products without damage). One who sees a certification mark on a product or in connection with a service is entitled to assume that that product or service in fact meets whatever standards of safety or quality have been established and advertised by the certifier.

In the United States, registration of collective membership marks and certification marks is conducted using the same general procedures as registration of traditional trademarks and service marks, although use and ownership requirements are slightly different. Application forms to register collective membership and certification marks with the USPTO can be found online at: http://www.uspto.gov/teas/eTEASpageA.htm.

Geographical Indications

Geographical indications (or GIs, as they are commonly called) are treated as a subset of trademarks in the United States. GIs identify a good or service as originating in a place, region, or locality where a given quality, reputation, or other characteristic of the good is essentially attributable to its geographic origin. Examples of GIs from the United States include FLORIDA for oranges, IDAHO for potatoes, VIDALIA for onions, and WASHINGTON STATE for apples. GIs are valuable to producers for the same reason that trademarks are valuable. They serve the same functions as trademarks because, like trademarks, they are source identifiers and guarantees of quality, and they represent valuable business interests.

GIs increasingly are being recognized as valuable marketing tools in the global economy. Further, intellectual property (IP) owners are finding that protecting IP is no longer just a domestic endeavor. Accordingly, IP owners need to be armed with information about domestic and foreign systems of GI protection in order to fully leverage the value added by GIs to their goods both at home and abroad.

Trademark Rights Applied to Domain Names

The distinction between Internet domain names and trademarks is important to understand. Generally speaking, a domain name serves as an address on the Internet, rather than as an indication of source for goods or services. In the vast majority of cases, therefore, domain names cannot be registered as trademarks.

A notable exception is the mark AMAZON.COM. In that case, the domain name also serves as a source identifier for online retail services. In contrast, the domain name www.barnesandnoble.com does not function as a trademark because the ".com" portion of the domain is not used as part of the company's brand. Rather, the well-known

book retailer uses the trademark BARNES & NOBLE, and the
domain www.barnesandnoble.com is used simply for an address on the Web.

Lesson 4: Patents

Introduction to Patents

Patented inventions touch every aspect of human life--from products that revolutionized industrial society, such as electric lighting, automobiles, and plastic, to products that have made life easier, such as dishwashers and ballpoint pens. By creating a system of economic reward in exchange for disclosure of knowledge, patent laws encourage the creation and distribution of products and technologies that enhance quality of life.

Definition of Patent

A patent is a Government grant of a property right that permits an inventor to exclude others from making, using, selling, offering for sale, or importing his or her invention. In return, the inventor must fully disclose the invention in the patent application process.

An invention is a product, machine, material or process, including a new use for a known product and improvements of any of these; that provides a new way of doing something or offers a new technical solution to a problem.

Patents may be obtained for a broad array of subject matter, including machines, tools, instruments, methods, systems, processes, compounds, formulations, and even plants and animals in some circumstances.

Patent Requirements

Inventions must generally meet three requirements in order to be patentable:

- Novelty

   In order for an invention to qualify for patent protection, it must be new or novel. In other words, it may not be part of the state of the art known at the time of invention or, in some countries, at the time of filing for patent protection. The state of the art includes everything that is available anywhere in the world to the public through technical journals, magazines, published papers, books, patent databases, or any other source. New uses or improvements to known processes, machines, or materials may also qualify as novel if that particular use or improvement is not already known by the public.

   A famous example of a patent being rejected on novelty grounds concerns a 1974 patent application by two inventors, Mr. Loren Covington and Mr. Howard Palmer. Mr. Covington and Mr. Palmer invented a metal alloy made primarily of titanium, but with small amounts of nickel and molybdenum. In addition, the inventors discovered that the iron content should be limited in order to achieve certain desirable properties in the alloy. The U.S. Patent and Trademark Office rejected the inventors' claims to the alloy on the grounds that the invention lacked novelty because a Russian article published 4 years earlier disclosed the claimed alloy.

– Non-obviousness

In order to be patentable, an invention must not have been obvious to a person of "ordinary skill" in the field at the time the invention was made. This ensures that patents are granted only for true contributions to the state of the art.

– Utility

In order to qualify for patent protection, an invention must have some useful purpose. An abstract idea with no practical application would not be patentable. The standard of "usefulness" is not hard to meet, as is illustrated by the following examples of patented devices:

- A motorized ice cream cone
- A wearable hamster cage
- A Santa Claus detector
- A diaper alarm
- A bird diaper

Duration of Patents

International agreements to which the United States is a party provide that the term of protection for utility patents shall be a minimum of 20 years from the date of the patent application. This 20-year term is sometimes lengthened, particularly in cases where the invention is subject to regulatory review before being granted marketing approval.

Typically, in order to maintain patent rights for the full term of protection, maintenance fees must be paid on a regular basis in each country where a patent has been granted. If the maintenance fees are not paid, the patent will cease to remain in force and the invention will fall into the public domain. For more information on maintenance fees, go to: http://www.uspto.gov/main/howtofees.htm.

Note that design and plant patents have different terms of protection in different countries. In the United States, design patents have a 14-year term and plant patents have a 20-year term.

Territoriality of Patents

Like trademark rights, patents are territorial (i.e., a U.S. patent is enforceable only in the United States, a Japanese patent is enforceable only in Japan).

In order to obtain patent rights in a particular country, typically an inventor must apply for and be granted a patent in accordance with that country's laws and procedures.

U.S. Law vs. Other Countries' Laws

U.S. inventors seeking to protect patent rights at home and abroad should be aware that U.S. patent law differs from the patent laws of most other countries in two significant respects:

1. **First to Invent vs. First to File:** The United States currently has a "first to invent" system, which means that a patent will be granted to the person or persons shown to be the first inventor(s) of the subject matter in question. This system differs from the systems of almost all other countries, which have a "first to file" system that awards the patent to the first person or persons to file a patent application regardless of who invented it first. The U.S. patent law may change in the near future to a first-to-file system in an effort to harmonize U.S. laws with international norms. Please check the U.S. PTO Web site for current information on patent reform legislation.
2. **Public Disclosure:** U.S. law allows a 1-year grace period from the date of public disclosure or certain uses or sales of an invention for the inventor to file a U.S. patent application. In the United States, public disclosure must be in writing. However, note that slides at private meetings can be considered publications, as can private correspondence. In contrast, some other countries bar an inventor from obtaining a patent if the invention has been publicly disclosed before a patent application is filed. One such region, notably, is Europe. Therefore, in order to preserve their rights in foreign countries, U.S. inventors should be cautious in deciding when and where to disclose their inventions and when to file applications abroad. In some jurisdictions, a nonconfidential disclosure to anyone, anywhere in the world, may be a bar to obtaining a patent.

Integrated Circuit Designs, Industrial Designs, and Plant Varieties

In addition to the patent protections that may apply, certain types of inventions may have qualities or characteristics that are eligible for different or additional intellectual property rights (IPR) protections. These unique categories of IPR protection include:

– Integrated circuit designs

   Integrated circuit designs are the designs or plans of integrated circuits used in electronic equipment. Circuit designs are usually highly complex, and the intellectual effort in creating an original circuit design may be considerable and of great value.

An integrated circuit or chip made from the plans is the key to the operation of all kinds of electronic devices from heart pacemakers to personal computers.

- Industrial designs (design patents)

An industrial design is the ornamental aspect of an article. The design may consist of three-dimensional features, such as the shape or surface of an article, or two-dimensional features, such as patterns, line, or color. Industrial designs are applied to a wide variety of products, such as technical and medical instruments, housewares, electrical appliances, jewelry, and shoes. Note that this type of intellectual property (IP) may be treated differently in different countries.

- Plant varieties

In the United States, legal protection for new plant varieties is provided under the Plant Variety Protection Act (PVPA). The PVPA is a voluntary program that provides patent-like rights to breeders, developers, and owners of plant varieties. The primary purpose of the PVPA is to ensure that developers of varieties will benefit from and be able to recover research costs associated with producing new plant varieties.

Lesson 5: Trade Secrets and Undisclosed Information

Introduction to Trade Secrets

One of the most famous trade secrets in the world, the formula for Coca-Cola, is kept in a heavily guarded vault and is known to only a few people within the company. Like The Coca-Cola Company, companies around the world guard their proprietary information very carefully, often spending millions to preserve the confidentiality of information that they believe gives them an advantage over their competitors. Global protection of trade secrets has been slow to develop but has been hastened significantly by the implementation of international agreements.

Trade secrets encompass an almost infinite spectrum of information, such as:

- Customer lists
- Supplier lists
- Financial data
- Product formulas
- Manufacturing processes
- Marketing strategies
- Computer source code
- Pricing information

Definition of Trade Secret

In a general sense, a trade secret is confidential information that has commercial value. Under international agreements, trade secrets are defined to include information that:

- Is secret

  International law defines secret information as that which is not "generally known among or readily accessible to persons within the circles that normally deal with the kind of information in question."

- Has commercial value because it is secret

  Commercial value does not just mean dollar value; it can include anything that gives a business an advantage over competitors.

- Has been subject to reasonable procedures designed to maintain its secrecy

Duration of Trade Secrets

Trade secrets may be protected indefinitely so long as the information remains secret. If the secret is revealed, trade secret protection ceases.

There are many ways in which trade secret information may lose its secrecy. The most common are:

- Disclosure by employees to competitors or the public at large
- Nonconfidential disclosure by the company
- Independent invention or discovery of the trade secret
- Reverse engineering by competitors

Reverse engineering is the process of taking something apart (e.g., a device, an electrical component) and analyzing its workings in detail, usually with the intent to construct a new or similar device or program.

For example, a manufacturer may purchase a machine and disassemble it to determine what its parts are, how it is constructed and how it works. If the machine or its parts are not protected by patent, the manufacturer may produce the parts and assemble them into a new machine similar to or the same as the one the manufacturer purchased. In addition, the manufacturer may choose to improve on the machine to produce a more competitive machine.

Reverse engineering is a lawful way to obtain a trade secret in most parts of the world.

Trade Secrets vs. Patents

In some cases, a company has valuable information that could be protected either by obtaining a patent or by maintaining the information as a trade secret. In the late 1800's, for example, The Coca-Cola Company elected secrecy instead of a patent on its soda formula. Refer to the information below for a comparison of trade secrets and patents.

- Trade Secrets
    - Information **must not** be disclosed to be protected
    - No need to register information for it to be protected
    - No limit on term of protection so long as secrecy is preserved
    - No guaranteed minimum term of protection; if secrets are disclosed or reverse engineered, rights may be lost
    - Information must have commercial value

- Patents
    - Information **must** be disclosed to be protected
    - Patent must be applied for and granted in each country where protection is desired
    - Maximum protection is 20 years from date of filing in most countries
    - Minimum of 20 years' protection from date of filing is guaranteed once patent has been issued
    - Invention must be novel, nonobvious, and useful

Laws Protecting Trade Secrets

In the United States, unauthorized commercial use of a trade secret by a third party is prohibited by state law. Most state laws are based upon model legislation called the Uniform Trade Secrets Act. In addition, a federal law called the Economic Espionage Act gives the Attorney General sweeping powers to criminally prosecute a person for appropriating trade secrets.

As the leading exporter of technology in the world, the United States has been working to strengthen international standards for the protection of trade secrets, and international agreements now require countries to enact laws protecting against theft of "undisclosed information."

Historically, trade secret laws have not been as developed internationally as in the United States, and some foreign countries have failed to provide effective remedies against trade secret theft.

Undisclosed Information

Another important area of protection is the requirement of government regulators responsible for approving marketing of pharmaceutical or agricultural chemical products to protect the undisclosed information supplied to them as part of their approval process.

As a condition for approving the marketing of pharmaceutical or agricultural chemical products, government agencies may require the submission of undisclosed test or other data. The production of this undisclosed information often involves considerable effort and expense.

Government agencies are obligated to protect this undisclosed information against disclosure and unfair commercial use. In the United States, this protection of undisclosed information extends for:

- 5 years for pharmaceutical products
- 10 years for agricultural chemical products

During these time periods, third parties will not be able to rely on this undisclosed information or on the marketing approval of that product when seeking to market competing products.

Many countries around the world have similar time periods for the protection of undisclosed information, though some do not provide specific time periods for protection against unfair commercial use.

Module 4: How to Obtain and Protect Your IPRs in the United States

Lesson 1: Introduction

Introduction

As a U.S.-based business, your first concern with respect to intellectual property rights (IPRs) will be how to obtain and protect those rights within the United States. Taking all steps available to maximize protection of IPRs—even those that can exist in the United States without registration—is strongly advised.

This module addresses the basic steps you need to take to obtain and protect the following IPRs in the United States:

- Copyrights
- Trademarks
- Patents
- Trade Secrets

This module also addresses other means of protecting IPRs in the United States, including entering into independent contractor agreements, recording registered trademarks and copyrights with U.S. Customs and Border Protection, protecting your supply chain, and protecting your IPRs at trade fairs. Keep in mind, however, that the laws and procedures pertaining to the acquisition and protection of IPRs in the United

States or any other country are complex, and you should consult with an attorney who specializes in that particular type of IPR to assist you in this process.

Lesson 2: Copyright

Introduction to Copyright Protection in the United States

Copyright protection in the United States does not depend upon registration or any other official procedures or formalities. Rather, a creative work is considered protected by copyright as soon as it is created, provided that it is:

- Original
- Fixed in a tangible form

Copyright registration does, however, afford significant benefits to copyright owners, and it is necessary before an owner of a work of U.S. origin can bring a copyright infringement lawsuit in a U.S. court. On the next several screens, you will learn about the benefits of copyright registration and the procedures for securing a registration.

Benefits of Copyright Registration

There are numerous benefits to securing a copyright registration in the United States. A copyright registration:

- Establishes a public record of ownership of the copyright.
- Creates a legal presumption of ownership of the copyright.
- Is necessary for a U.S. rights holder to bring a lawsuit for copyright infringement of U.S. works in U.S. Federal courts.
- Strengthens a copyright owner's position in a copyright infringement court case.
- Is necessary to record the copyright with U.S. Customs to prevent infringing imports from entering the country.
- Allows the copyright owner to claim statutory damages and attorney's fees in a copyright infringement suit. (Otherwise, the owner must prove actual damages and pay his or her own attorney's fees.)

Copyright registration is available for unpublished as well as published works.

Procedures for Registering a Copyright

Copyright registration in the United States is relatively straightforward. To register a copyright, the owner must:

- Complete the appropriate application form for the specific type of work
    o Forms are available at www.copyright.gov/register
    o Detailed instructions are included with each form

- For help with completing applications, go to www.copyright.gov/circs/circ1c.pdf
- Send the application to: Library of Congress, Copyright Office, 101 Independence Avenue, S.E., Washington, DC 20559-6000, together with a:
  - $45 filing fee
  - Non-returnable copy (or copies) of the material to be registered (the deposit) as specified in the detailed instructions for that form

The nature of the deposit required to register a copyright depends upon the nature of the work to be registered and is set forth in the detailed instructions with the form for that work. For example:

- For *two-dimensional works* (e.g., a cartoon or greeting card), a copy of the work is required.
- For *three-dimensional works* (e.g., a sculpture or toy), identifying material" is required, such as photographs, drawings, or other two-dimensional reproductions of the work.

For more information about copyright deposit requirements in the United States, go to http://www.copyright.gov/circs/circ40a.html#three.

For more information on copyright registration, visit www.copyright.gov/help/faq/.

Use of a Copyright Notice

In addition to securing a copyright registration, another step that U.S. copyright owners take to protect their work is affixing a copyright notice to their work, even when their work is not published.

"Publication" has a technical meaning in copyright law. Generally, publication occurs on the date on which copies of the work are first made available to the public. Publication is important because:

- Works that are published in the United States are subject to mandatory deposit with the Library of Congress
- Publication of a work can affect the limitations on the exclusive rights of the copyright owner
- The year of publication may determine the duration of copyright protection for anonymous and pseudonymous works (when the author's identity is not revealed in the records of the Copyright Office) and for works made for hire
- Deposit requirements for registration of published works differ from those for registration of unpublished works
- When a work is published, it may bear a notice of copyright to identify the year of publication and the name of the copyright owner and to inform the public that the work is protected by copyright

Like copyright registration, use of the copyright notice is not required, but it does afford the copyright owner certain benefits such as:

- Informing the public that the work is protected by copyright, thus deterring infringement
- Informing the public of the name of the copyright owner and the year of first publication of the work
- Eliminating the potential for use of the "innocent infringement" defense in court

In a copyright infringement case, infringers often raise the defense of "innocent infringement"--that is, that he or she did not realize that his or her acts constituted infringement of copyright. An innocent infringement defense may result in a reduction in damages that the copyright owner would otherwise receive. If a work has a proper copyright notice, however, the court will not give any weight to a defendant's innocent infringement defense.

It is important to note that copyright registration is not required to use the copyright notice.

Proper Use of Copyright Notice

A copyright notice should contain three elements:

1. The symbol © (the letter C in a circle) or the word "Copyright"
2. The year of first publication
3. The name of the copyright owner of the work

Example for published works: © 2007 Jane Doe

Example for unpublished works: Unpublished work © 2007 Jane Doe

Use of a copyright notice on copies of the unpublished work that leave the owner's control may be useful in deterring infringement. Similarly, unpublished works may be registered with the Copyright Office.

Some people like to add contact information to their copyright notice so that interested parties know how to contact them to obtain permission to use their works. A statement regarding the owner's copyright rights is also included sometimes, either as a reminder or cautionary note or to spell out the owner's licensing of his or her rights (e.g., "All rights reserved").

Protecting Your Web site

Most businesses today have a Web site for the purpose of transacting business through the Internet and/or to provide information to potential consumers. Whether your Web site supports e-commerce or is simply informational, there are IPRs that are important to protect. As the value and reputation of your business grows, so does the risk that others may steal the content, graphics or general "look and feel" of your Web site. Most elements of a Web site are protected by copyright law, for example:

- Text
- Graphics
- Photographs
- Code
- Compilations of data
- Video and audio recordings
- Arrangement and selection of any of the above

If you have taken proper steps to ensure ownership of the copyright in these elements of your Web site, they can be protected through the means discussed in this course for protecting other creative works, such as copyright registration and use of a copyright notice.

As you learned in the previous lesson, at least in the United States, you do not own the copyright in material created by an independent contractor unless you have a written agreement stating that the work is a work made for hire or, if it is not a work made for hire, transferring the copyright to you. Therefore, if you hire a Web site developer to create your Web site for you, you need to have a proper website development agreement in place to ensure that you will own all IPRs in the Web site. More information regarding Web site development agreements can be found through several free resources on the Web, one of which is http://www.wipo.int/sme/en/documents/business_website.htm

In addition to stealing copyrighted works, others may steal the trademarks for registration and use in their own country or for domain names. For these reasons, most Web site owners maintain links on their Web sites to detailed information about their intellectual property (IP) and about any third-party IP that they may have licensed for use.

More information on protecting IPRs in your Web site is available through many free resources available on the web, one of which is http://www.wipo.int/sme/en/documents/business_website.htm.

Lesson 3: Trademarks

Introduction to Trademark Protection in the United States

As with copyrights, protection of trademarks in the United States does not depend upon registration. However, trademark registration provides significant benefits for the trademark owner and is strongly recommended as a vital step in strong international enforcement. On the next several screens, you will learn about the benefits of trademark registration and the procedures for securing a registration.

Procedures for Selecting Trademarks in the United States

Before selecting a trademark, you should conduct searches to determine whether a proposed mark is available for use. There is no guarantee, however, that searches will identify all possible conflicts. The exercise is one of assessing the level of business risk associated with adopting any particular mark and choosing a mark that has minimal risk. U.S. businesses or individuals seeking to conduct trademark searches should contact an experienced trademark attorney to assist with this process.

A preliminary search of proposed word and design marks may be conducted in the U.S. Patent and Trademark Office's (USPTO's) Trademark Electronic Search System (TESS). This database contains federally registered marks and pending applications for Federal trademark registration. As the United States is a first to use country, you also may wish to search the Web to see whether there is any evidence that a proposed mark is already in use. Be aware, however, that these preliminary searches should not be relied upon as determinative of a mark's availability. Rather, if preliminary searches show no likely conflicts, a "full" search should be conducted.

Professional search firms, which have expertise in conducting trademark searches, are used to conduct full trademark searches. Such firms have access to proprietary databases and other sources of trademarks that are registered and/or in use.
The full search is designed to identify possible conflicts with federally registered marks and pending applications, state registrations, common law marks, and domain names.
The results of a full search generally are reviewed and evaluated by a trademark attorney.

Benefits of Trademark Registration

In the United States, unlike in many other countries, trademark rights are established through use of a trademark in the United States in connection with goods or services. If there is a dispute between two parties regarding a particular trademark, the party who used the mark first will prevail even if the other party obtained a registration for the mark first.

Although trademark registration is not required in the United States, the benefits of registering a mark are significant. A U.S. trademark registration provides:

- Constructive notice to the public of the registrant's claim of ownership of the mark
- A legal presumption of the registrant's ownership of the mark and the registrant's exclusive right to use the mark nationwide on or in connection with the goods and/or services listed in the registration
- The ability to bring an action concerning the mark in Federal court
- A basis for obtaining a trademark registration in foreign countries
- The ability to file the U.S. registration with U.S. Customs and Border Protection to prevent importation of infringing foreign goods
- The right to use the registered trademark symbol (®) with the trademark

A trademark owner must use his or her mark in a particular territory in order to have trademark protection under common law. By securing a Federal trademark registration, however, the trademark owner obtains a presumption of exclusive trademark ownership nationwide, even in areas where he or she has not yet used the mark. Nationwide priority is frequently cited as the most important benefit of trademark registration because it eliminates the risk of others establishing rights in the same trademark before the business has been able to expand its use of the mark nationwide.

The following example illustrates the benefits of nationwide priority afforded by federal trademark registration:

Sally Jones has dreams of owning a nationwide chain of old-fashioned malt shops. She begins with one malt shop in Small Town, Wisconsin, that she calls "Memory Lane Malts." She does not secure a trademark registration for the mark "Memory Lane Malts." One year later, Debbie Dover opens an old-fashioned ice cream parlor called "Memory Lane Sweets" in Topeka, Kansas. Debbie is not aware of Sally's "Memory Lane Malts" shop. Both Sally and Debbie have success with their businesses, and each opens a few more shops in their respective states. After 5 years, Sally secures financing to expand her malt shops nationwide. She becomes aware of Debbie's ice cream parlors and is very upset. She hires an attorney, who tells her that because she does not have a Federal trademark registration, there is nothing Sally can do to prevent Debbie from using the "Memory Lane Sweets" mark in the places where Debbie already has shops.

So what could Sally have done initially in light of her plans for a nationwide chain? At the outset, Sally could have filed an intent-to-use (ITU) trademark application based upon her good faith intention to use the mark in commerce. Then, had Debbie checked the USPTO database prior to using her "Memory Lane Sweets" mark, she would have seen Sally's application to register "Memory Lane Malts" for related services and likely would have been deterred from using the "Memory Lane Sweets" mark. Had Debbie chosen to use the "Memory Lane Sweets" mark in spite of Sally's trademark application, upon registration of Sally's "Memory Lane Malts" mark, Sally could have sued Debbie to stop her from using the "Memory Lane Sweets" mark.

What can Sally do now? Sally could consider filing an application for Federal registration that, if granted, would limit Debbie's ability to expand geographically beyond the places where Debbie currently has shops.

You may file your trademark application online using the Trademark Electronic Application System (TEAS), which can be found at: http://uspto.gov/teas/index.html

State trademark registration also offers certain benefits. Each of the 50 states operates a trademark office within the secretary of state's office. Applicants may find obtaining a state trademark registration to be cheaper and less time consuming than a federal trademark registration.

However, the effect and value of state registrations can vary dramatically from state to state. For example, some state registrations grant no rights that you do not already possess under common law without registration. While some state registration laws merely provide that a certificate of state registration as proof of registration in the state, other states may give a registration greater evidentiary effect regarding ownership and/or validity of the trademark.

State registration limits rights to within state's borders, whereas federal registration protects you in all states. If you will be using your trademark in more than one state, you should consider federal registration.

Procedures for Registering Trademarks in the United States

Trademark applications, like trademark searches, can be complex, and the assistance of experienced trademark counsel is generally advised. If you are considering filing a trademark application without an attorney's assistance, you will want to review the materials on the USPTO Web site (www.uspto.gov) and familiarize yourself with the following aspects of trademark applications:

– Use-based vs. Intend-to-use (ITU) applications

In the United States, most trademark applications are use-based – that is, a trademark has already been used in connection with a product or service. In these situations, a "use-based" application can be filed. A use-based application must include a sworn declaration that the mark is in use in commerce and must list the date of first use of the mark anywhere and the date of first use of the mark in commerce. Use in commerce is defined by the trademark law as placement of the mark on products or services plus interstate or international sale or transportation of the products or services. A properly worded declaration is included in the USPTO standard application form. More information is available online for help in establishing use.

In the United States, it is possible to file an application to register a trademark even before the mark has actually been used. If you have not yet used a trademark but intend to do so in the future, you can file an ITU application to register the mark. An ITU application must include a sworn declaration that you have a bona fide intention to use the mark in commerce. A properly worded declaration is included in the application form provided by the USPTO. Note that if you file based on ITU, you must begin actually using of the mark in commerce before the USPTO will register the mark; that is, after filing an application based on ITU, you must later file another form (an Allegation of Use form or a Statement of Use form) to establish that use in commerce has begun.

The advantage of filing an ITU application can be considerable. Upon registration, the registrant may use the filing date of the application as the constructive use date. This date can be used to defeat those who use the same or a similar mark for related goods or services at a later date. Thus, by filing an ITU application, a business can reserve a mark while it continues to develop its plans for introducing the product or service into the marketplace. However, no registration can be issued until the applicant provides acceptable evidence of use.

- Description of goods and/or services

Trademarks are used in connection with goods or services. Thus, a trademark application must include a statement identifying the goods and/or services with which the mark is used or will be used. The identification of goods and/or services must be specific enough to identify the nature of the goods and/or services. For examples of acceptable identifications, go to the USPTO Trademark Acceptable Identification of Goods and Services at: http://tess2.uspto.gov/netahtml/tidm.html.

A trademark attorney can help your business by ensuring that the description is accurate and sufficiently broad to maximize protection of the mark.

- Specimens showing use of the mark

A use-based trademark application must include a "specimen," which is an actual example of how the mark is being used in connection with the identified goods and/or services. An ITU application does not require a specimen (because the mark has not yet been used), but you would need to file a specimen with the Allegation of Use form or Statement of Use form evidencing use of the mark with the goods or services, which is required before an ITU application can proceed to registration.

For marks used in connection with goods (products), the specimen should show the mark on the actual goods or packaging for the goods. You may submit a tag or label for the goods, a container for the goods, a display associated with the goods, or a photograph of the goods that shows use of the mark on the goods. You should not submit the actual product.

For marks used in connection with services, the specimen should show the mark used in the sale of or advertising for the services. You may submit a sign, a brochure about the services, an advertisement for the services, a business card or stationery showing the mark in connection with the services, or a photograph showing the mark as used in rendering or advertising the services. There must be some reference to the type of services rendered on the specimen (i.e., not just a display of the mark itself). For example, if the mark sought to be registered is "XYZ," a business card that shows only the mark "XYZ" would not be acceptable. A business card that states "XYZ REAL ESTATE" as a specimen of the XYZ mark for real estate services would be acceptable.

- Depiction of the mark (the "drawing")

Every application must include a clear drawing of the mark you want to register. If you are preparing the drawing page yourself, use white, non-shiny paper that is 8½ inches wide by 11 inches long. The mark can be no larger than 3.5 inches high by 3.5 inches wide. The drawing page should include a heading with the following elements:

- o The applicant's name
- o The correspondence address
- o A listing of goods and/or services
- o Dates of use (if already using the mark in commerce) or the wording "Intent to Use"

The representation of the mark must then appear below the heading in the middle of the page and in the proper format for either a "standard character" drawing or a "stylized or special form" drawing. Once filed, you cannot make a material change to your mark.

To see examples of proper drawing pages, go to: http://www.uspto.gov/web/offices/tac/doc/basic/appcontent.htm#dep.

– Paper application vs. online filing

You may file your trademark application online using the Trademark Electronic Application System (TEAS), which can be found at: http://uspto.gov/teas/index.html. TEAS allows you to fill out an application form and submit it directly to the USPTO over the Internet. If you file online through TEAS, you will receive a summary of the filing by e-mail and your application will be assigned an immediate serial number. Today, almost all new trademark applications are filed directly over the Internet using TEAS.

Filing through TEAS also enables you to lower your filing fee. If you file a paper application, the cost is $375 per class of goods or services. Using TEAS, however, lowers your fee to $325. And if you file using TEAS Plus, in which you agree to accept communications via e-mail during the pendency of your application, you can lower your fee per class to $275. To determine whether to use TEAS or TEAS Plus, go to: http://teasplus.uspto.gov/TeasPlus/.

To file a paper application, send it by regular mail to:

Commissioner for Trademarks
P.O. Box 1451
Alexandria, VA 22313-1451

Paper forms are not processed as quickly as those submitted electronically, and you should allow at least 2 to 3 weeks to receive a filing receipt for your application.

- Application fees

  Trademark application fees vary depending upon the type of application and the method of filing. You may obtain the current schedule of fees at http://www.uspto.gov/go/fees/index.html.

Trademark Examination Process

After a trademark application is filed, it goes through an examination process that can take 18 months or longer to complete. The process consists of the following steps:

- o Office Action

  If there are problems with the application, the examining attorney issues an Office Action stating the grounds for initial refusal of the application (e.g., that the mark is confusingly similar to another mark already registered or applied for, or that the mark is not sufficiently distinctive to function as a trademark or that the description of goods or services is unacceptable).

- o Response to Office Action

  The applicant has 6 months to respond to the Office Action. In the response, the applicant can either refute the examining attorney's arguments or amend the application. The examining attorney then reviews the applicant's response and either accepts the response or issues a final refusal to register the mark.

- o Published for Opposition

  If the application is approved, it is published for opposition in a USPTO publication called "The Official Gazette." An opposition may be filed by anyone who believes he or she would be damaged by issuance of the registration. If an opposition is filed, the applicant and the party opposing the registration engage in an administrative proceeding before the USPTO Trademark Trial and Appeal Board (TTAB) to determine whether the registration should be granted.

- o Allowance of Registration

  If there no opposition is filed by a third party, the USPTO issues either a Certificate of Registration or a Notice of Allowance (depending on whether the application is use based or ITU).

Maintenance of Trademark Registrations

A Federal trademark registration can last indefinitely if the owner continues to use the mark in connection with the goods and/or services and files all the necessary documentation with the USPTO at the appropriate times. In general, the owner of a registration must file:

- o Affidavits of Continued Use or Excusable Nonuse (Section 8 Affidavit) between years 5 and 6 following registration

  Between the fifth and sixth year anniversary of the registration of the mark, a Section 8 Affidavit must be filed in order to maintain the registration. The Section 8 Affidavit states that the mark is still in use. A specimen showing current use of the mark must accompany the affidavit when filed with the USPTO. If a Section 8 Affidavit is not filed before the sixth anniversary of the registration date or within the 6-month grace period (late fees apply), the registration is canceled.

  If the mark is not in use but the owner believes the registration should not be canceled, then it is necessary to submit the affidavit stating that the mark is not in use along with a statement that there are special circumstances which excuse the nonuse and that the nonuse is not due to any intention to abandon the mark.

- o A Renewal Application between years 9 and 10 following registration

  Within a 1-year period prior to the 10th anniversary of the registration date, a renewal application must be filed with the USPTO in order to maintain the registration. The renewal application must include a Section 9 Affidavit stating that the mark is still in use as well as a specimen showing current use of the mark. There is a 6-month grace period after the tenth anniversary during which a renewal application will be accepted upon payment of an additional fee. Each renewal term is 10 years. Failure to renew results in cancellation of the registration.

Forms for filing these documents are available at http://www.uspto.gov/teas/. Failure to file these documents will result in loss of the Federal registration, but not in the loss of the underlying trademark rights, unless the owner fails to maintain those rights in the manner discussed on the following screen.

Maintenance of Trademark Rights

Because trademark rights in the United States are not dependent upon registration, maintenance of trademark registrations is not the same as maintenance of trademark rights. Trademark rights are maintained through continuous and proper use of the mark and enforcement of rights in the mark. Failure to follow these steps could result in abandonment of trademark rights:

- Continuous use of the mark

  Trademark rights must be maintained through actual use of the trademark in connection with goods or services. In the United States, nonuse of a trademark for 3 consecutive years is considered to be presumptive evidence that the mark has been abandoned. (This evidence can be overcome by the trademark owner in some cases, but you do not want to be in the position of having to prove that you have not abandoned your trademark).

- Consistent and proper use of the mark

  In addition to ensuring that a mark is used continuously, it is also important to ensure that a mark is used:

  o **Consistently.** The mark must be used in a manner that is consistent with the trademark registration. If a mark is materially changed, a new registration should be secured. For example, suppose a bank establishes trademark rights in the mark CHASE SMARTCARD for a credit card offering cash-back dividends. After a few years, the company's marketing team decides to shorten the mark to CHASECARD. Use of the mark CHASECARD will not preserve rights in the mark CHASE SMARTCARD. If the original mark is registered, a new application to register the new mark CHASECARD should be filed. The same principles apply to logos (such as Nike's "Swoosh" logo). As a logo is updated over time, new registrations must be secured if the changes to the mark are material.

  o **Properly.** The mark must always be used as an adjective, never as a noun or a verb. Using the mark as a noun or a verb, or allowing others to do so, could result in the mark becoming generic. A classic example is the mark XEROX. Over time, consumers began to use the mark as a verb ("I need to xerox some documents"), which required the company to engage in an extensive public relations campaign advising consumers to "photocopy" instead of "xerox" documents. These efforts failed to preserve the mark in Russia, Bulgaria and Romania. One way to help avoid a mark becoming generic is to follow the trademark with the word "brand." For example, Johnson & Johnson changed the lyrics of its Band-Aid television commercial jingle from, "*I am stuck on Band-Aids, 'cause Band-Aid's stuck on me*" to "*I am stuck on Band-Aid **brand**, 'cause Band-Aid's stuck on me.*"

  o **With appropriate trademark notices.** As discussed on the following screen, it is not uncommon in the United States to use the symbols TM (trademark) and SM (service mark) in connection with marks that are not registered and the symbol ® in connection with marks that are registered.

- Enforcement of rights in the mark

  Trademark owners must take action against third parties who, without their consent, use a mark that is confusingly similar to their mark. Failure to police infringers can progressively weaken the mark's strength and may, over time, cause the mark to be declared abandoned.

  Trademark owners should take affirmative steps to monitor the market for infringing uses of their trademarks. This can be done by periodically searching the Internet for uses of the mark, attending trade fairs, and utilizing trademark monitoring services. Trademark monitoring services can watch for marks being applied for or registered and used in foreign countries as well as in the United States. Also, the USPTO Official Gazette is available at the USPTO website at http://www.uspto.gov/web/trademarks/tmog/.

  If an infringing use of a trademark is discovered, the trademark owner should undertake efforts to stop the infringement.

- Proper licensing contracts and oversight

  Trademark owners licensing the right to use their mark to third parties (e.g. manufacturers, distributors, etc.) should ensure that the license agreement is in writing. In addition, trademark owners must exercise quality control over the licensee's products and/or services. Failure to exercise proper quality control over licensees' use of an owner's mark also could result in the trademarks being declared abandoned.

- Centralized control of the mark

  Each trademark owner, assuming it is composed of corporate entity or more than one person, should designate a specific person to be charged with oversight of trademark matters. That person should work closely with trademark counsel in developing trademark programs, reviewing and making decisions concerning trademark availability searches, determining the breadth of the trademark portfolio, ensuring that the business's marks are properly licensed (and that the business also has permission to use others' marks), addressing problems with the trademark program as they arise, and overseeing actions to enforce trademark rights against third parties.

Use of Trademark Symbols

In the United States, businesses sometimes use certain trademark symbols in connection with public display of their marks as a means of alerting the public that rights are claimed in those marks. The proper symbol to use depends upon whether or not the trademark is registered:

- The symbols TM (trademark) and SM (service mark) may be used in connection with any mark to put others on notice of a claim of rights in the mark.
- The symbol ® may be used only in connection with marks that are registered with the USPTO.

Because there is no universal symbol for trademark registration, some businesses operating in more than one country prefer to use a statement describing their rights (e.g., "TRADEMARK is a registered mark of [owner] in the United States and other countries") rather than a trademark symbol so that packaging and marketing materials do not need to be revised for distribution in different countries.

Lesson 4: Patents

Introduction to Patent Protection in the United States

Unlike copyright and trademark protection, patent protection in the United States is dependent upon registration. Unless a patent is granted, patent rights in an invention are not generally protected. General information on patent protection is provided on the following screens. Keep in mind, however, that patent registration is extremely complex and should not be attempted without the assistance of an experienced patent attorney. Introduction to Patent Protection in the United States

Types of Patents

The U.S. Patent and Trademark Office (USPTO) issues three kinds of patents:

- **Utility patent** (20-year term of protection). This patent is the type most people think of when they talk about patents — protection for technological advances and innovation. A utility patent can be granted for any of the following or an improvement on any of them:
   o A manufactured article, such as a waffle maker or a vacuum cleaner
   o A machine, such as a photocopier or a computer
   o A composition of matter, such as a medicine or a carpet cleaner
   o A process for making or doing something, such as a method for refining oil
- **Design patent** (14- year term of protection). This patent covers a new and original ornamental design for a manufactured article. The shape or ornamentation can have no functional utility other than an aesthetic one. For example, the shape of a table lamp or an automobile body may be protected by a design patent.
- **Plant patent** (20-year term of protection). This patent may be granted by USPTO to anyone who invents or discovers any distinct and new plant variety that has been asexually reproduced by grafting or selective cuttings (without seed manipulation).

Note that plant patents differ from plant **variety protection**. New varieties of plants that are sexually reproduced by seed or are tuber-propagated can be protected under the Plant Variety Protection Act (PVPA). The PVPA is administered by the U.S. Department of Agriculture, and information about the PVPA can be found at: http://www.ams.usda.gov/Science/PVPA/PVPindex.htm.

Public Disclosure of Patent Prior to Application

U.S. law allows a 1-year grace period after public disclosure or certain uses or sales of an invention to file a patent application. In the United States, disclosure of an invention is generally deemed to occur when the invention has been made sufficiently available to the interested public.

In contrast, many other countries bar an inventor from obtaining a patent if the invention has been publicly disclosed before a patent application is filed. Therefore, in order to preserve patent rights in foreign countries, inventors should be cautious in deciding when to disclose inventions and when to file applications abroad.

How to Protect an Invention When Pitching It

Inventors who are not in a position to independently commercialize an idea are often faced with a dilemma. To make money from the invention, they generally must license the rights to another business, such as a manufacturer or distributor. But in pitching the invention to potential licensees, the inventor runs the risk that the invention may be stolen or no longer protected by law because it has been publicly disclosed.

Unfortunately, if an invention has not yet been patented, the risks associated with pitching it are significant, and it is impossible to fully eliminate them. As with most intellectual property (IP) matters, it is generally advisable to consult with an experienced IP attorney before proceeding. An IP attorney may suggest a variety of strategies, such as:

- Filing a provisional patent application

    If your invention potentially qualifies for a patent, you may consider filing a provisional application for a patent. Filing a provisional patent application, which is relatively easy and inexpensive. Having a provisional application on file will enable you to claim "patent pending" status, a claim which may provide some deterrent to possible infringement.

- Using nondisclosure agreements

    Another way to protect yourself when pitching an idea is to have prospective licensees sign a nondisclosure agreement before you disclose any confidential information. If someone signs a nondisclosure agreement and later uses the confidential information you disclosed without authorization, you can sue for damages.

You should be aware, however, that large corporations usually have IP or licensing departments specifically set up to handle and manage the inflow of product licensing opportunities. Many of these offices will not accept any submission of a licensing opportunity for which a patent has not yet been issued. Further, many will not sign a confidentiality agreement at all, while many others will be willing to sign only their own agreement, which generally will have terms that are not favorable to you. Thus, it is advisable when pitching an idea to know the person or company to which you are making the pitch and, in any event, to limit what you disclose.

- Keeping an invention notebook

    You can also protect the rights to your idea by thoroughly documenting the dates and milestones related to its creation. You would need to take this step during the process of developing your idea, well in advance of pitching it. Many attorneys advise their clients to keep an invention notebook in which the inventor records the things he or she did and tried to do that led to the development of the invention. It is also a good idea to periodically have the notebook notarized so that you can prove the dates associated with the creation of the idea in court in the event the idea is stolen after you pitch it.

Procedures for Obtaining a U.S. Patent

Because of the complexity of the patent application process, the first step toward obtaining a U.S. patent is generally the hiring of a patent attorney. The USPTO Web site contains a list of registered patent attorneys by geographic region at http://des.uspto.gov/OEDCI/.

A patent attorney will assist the inventor with the two basic steps necessary to obtain a patent:

- Conducting a search of prior art

    An invention may be patented if it is new, useful and non-obvious to one of ordinary skill in the art. The "prior art" (i.e., the body of knowledge existing prior to the invention) helps determine whether or not the invention is new and non-obvious. In other words, a prior art search reveals whether or not an invention has already been patented.

    Patent attorneys are experienced in conducting prior art searches using resources such as scientific publications, the Internet, and the U.S. patent database.

- Completing and filing a patent application

A U.S. patent application must include:

- A description of the invention, usually accompanied by drawings, plans, or diagrams
- Specific claims that indicate the scope of protection being sought in the patent

The fees associated with a patent application vary depending on the nature of the applicant (individuals pay less than large corporations) and the number of claims made in the application. A schedule of current patent fees can be found at http://www.uspto.gov/main/howtofees.htm. Depending upon the nature of the technology involved, the patent examination process can take anywhere from 2 to 4 years to complete.

Examination of a patent application by the USPTO follows these basic steps:

After being assigned a patent application, the USPTO examiner checks if the application is patentable and, more precisely, if the patent application:

- Complies with patent writing rules
- Has a patentable (statutory) subject matter
- Enables a person of the art to implement the invention
- Is useful, novel, and inventive
- Has claims that are supported by the description

If the examiner finds that the invention is not patentable (i.e., it does not meet at least one of the criteria described above), the following steps are taken:

1. The examiner issues a written rejection of the application, explaining the reasons for the rejection and possibly suggesting changes. Depending upon the reasons for the rejection, the examiner may also suggest abandoning the application.

2. The applicant replies to the rejection in a document usually entitled "Remarks." The applicant may also amend the application, which usually consists of changes to the patent claims but can also include descriptions or abstract changes.

3. The examiner analyzes the applicant's answer. If the examiner still considers the invention to be not patentable, he or she makes another rejection, to which to the applicant may again reply. When, and if, the examiner makes a final determination that the invention is not patentable, he or she issues a final rejection.

If the examiner finds that the application is patentable, he or she issues a Notice of Allowance, after which a patent is issued.

While an application is pending, a notice of "patent pending" can be placed on marketing materials or the goods themselves to notify the public that an application has been filed, but there is no legal protection for the patent during this period.

For more information on patent applications, go to
http://www.uspto.gov/main/patents.htm.

To see an example of a U.S. patent application, go to
http://www.uspto.gov/patft/index.html.

Provisional Patent Applications

Since 1995, the USPTO has offered inventors the option of filing a provisional application for utility patents. The provisional patent application was designed as a simpler and less expensive way for inventors to get an application on file and begin the process of protecting an invention. A provisional patent allows filing without any formal patent claims or any information disclosure (prior art) statement. The provisional patent application was intended to provide the time to further develop and fine-tune the invention and to save inventors from unnecessarily spending thousands of dollars on a full utility patent application until after they were more technically and/or financially ready to complete the requirements.

The provisional application provides the means to establish an early effective filing date, which may be important in establishing the priority of the invention over other similar inventions or in defining what prior art will be compared to the invention during examination of the full utility patent. However, it is important to understand that a provisional patent application provides no legal protection for the invention, is itself never examined, and acts only as a "placeholder" for the full utility application. If a utility application is not filed within the year, the provisional application is abandoned, and the inventor can no longer benefit from the earlier filing date.

Maintenance of Patents

Patents are subject to the payment of maintenance fees to maintain the patent in force. These fees are due at 3½, 7½ and 11½ years from the date the patent is granted and can be paid without a surcharge during the "window period," which is the 6-month period preceding each due date (e.g., 3 years to 3 years 6 months).

Failure to pay the current maintenance fee on time may result in expiration of the patent. A 6-month grace period is provided when the maintenance fee may be paid with a surcharge. The USPTO does not mail notices to patent owners that maintenance fees are due.

A current schedule of patent maintenance fees can be found at:
http://www.uspto.gov/main/howtofees.htm.

Lesson 5: Trade Secrets

Introduction to Trade Secret Protection in the United States

Unlike copyrights, trademarks, and patents, there is no procedure for registering trade secrets in the United States. There are, however, many steps that you can and should take to ensure that your trade secrets are protected.

In the United States, protection of trade secrets is governed by state law rather than Federal law.

Methods of Protecting Trade Secrets

Because trade secret protection is lost when secrecy is lost, companies must make concerted efforts to prevent their proprietary business information from becoming public. Some of the ways companies can protect trade secrets are:

- Mark documents and data that contain trade secret information "confidential."
- Limit the number of people who know the information and have access to confidential documents and data.
- Ensure that no one person knows all the confidential information.
- Restrict access to the information (keep it locked in a secure place; use computer encryption, passwords, and network security).
- Have the people who know the information agree in writing not to disclose it (by signing nondisclosure agreements).
- Include treatment of confidential and trade secret information in employee manuals.

Non-Disclosure Agreements

A nondisclosure agreement (also called an NDA or a confidentiality agreement) is a contract in which the parties promise to protect the confidentiality of secret information that is disclosed during employment or another type of business transaction. If you make a nondisclosure agreement with someone who uses your secret without authorization, you can request a court to stop the violator from making any further disclosures and you can sue for damages.

Lesson 6: Other Means of Protecting IPRs in the United States

Introduction to Other Means of Protecting IPRs in the U.S.

In addition to registering intellectual property (IP) and using appropriate IP symbols and notices, there are other steps you can take to protect your intellectual property rights (IPRs) in the United States. These steps include:

- Entering into written agreements with independent contractors regarding ownership of IPRs and nondisclosure of confidential information
- Recording registered trademarks and registered copyrights with U.S. Customs and Border Protection (CBP)
- Protecting your supply chain

Entering Into Independent Contractor Agreements

During the development of a new product or a new business, companies often employ the services of independent contractors. For example, a graphic artist may be hired to create a new logo for a business or an engineer may be hired to help develop the prototype of a new invention. A common trap some IP owners fall into is to outsource to independent contractors without ensuring that:

- There is a written contractor agreement
- The agreement contains provisions regarding:
  o Ownership of IP generated by the contractor
  o Nondisclosure of confidential information

Without the protection of a contractor agreement, the independent contractor could end up owning important parts of the IP or could disclose confidential information to third parties about the business or invention. Accordingly, it is critical that a written contractor agreement accompany the hiring of any independent contractor.

A written contractor agreement should:

- State that any IP developed by the contractor will be owned by the business or individual hiring the contractor and specifically transfer any copyright therein to the business
- Require the contractor to maintain confidentiality of both the IP disclosed in order for the contract work to be done and the IP generated by the contractor

Recording Trademarks and Copyrights With CBP

IP owners face a significant and growing problem of counterfeit and pirated goods being manufactured in foreign countries and exported to the United States. If possible, it is best to use the court system in the foreign country where the infringing goods are being manufactured to stop the infringement at its source. Unfortunately, enforcement at the source in other countries often can be difficult.

As an additional tool to help IP owners address the problem of IP theft, CBP has established border enforcement procedures to prevent the entry of infringing goods into domestic commerce. CBP's border enforcement procedures can be used to prevent the import of:

– Counterfeit trademark goods

Counterfeit trademark goods are essentially fakes; that is, products that are packaged to appear as though they have been manufactured by or with the consent of a trademark owner when they have not. For example, sunglasses bearing the RAY BAN trademark that are not manufactured by or with the consent of the owner of the RAY BAN mark would be considered counterfeit.

– Pirated copyright goods

Piracy refers to the unauthorized use, copying, and/or distribution of copyrighted material. The most common pirated goods are computer software, CDs, and DVDs.

CBP's border enforcement procedures cannot be used to prevent the import of products that infringe patent rights. A process called a Section 337 investigation does exist to address this problem.

How to Record Trademarks and Copyrights With Customs

In order to benefit from the border enforcement procedures, it is highly advisable to record trademark and copyrights with CBP. This enables CBP to monitor shipments and intercept imports and exports of infringing goods. Trademarks and copyrights can be recorded with CBP online at: http://www.cbp.gov/xp/cgov/import/commercial_enforcement/ipr/.

For each recordation, you will need:

- An application completed online.
- A digital image of the protected work in either .jpg or .gif format (limited to 2MB).
- $190 fee payment (good for 10 years' protection).
- A copy of the U.S. Patent and Trademark Office (USPTO) Certificate of Registration or additional photocopies of the status copy of the copyrighted work. (These are not required in every case but you may be asked to provide them.)

Once approved, your rights will be included in CBP's national database, accessible by CBP officers at over 300 ports nationwide. If you have questions or need assistance, CBP IPR paralegals are available at iprrquestions@dhs.gov or 202-572-8710.

If you choose not to use the online system for recording trademarks and copyrights with CBP, you can mail hard copies of necessary documentation to:

U.S. Customs and Border Protection / Office of Regulations & Rulings
Attention: Chief, Intellectual Property Rights Branch
Mint Annex Building
1300 Pennsylvania Avenue, NW
Washington, DC 20229

Note that paper recordations require extensive handling and are usually not approved as quickly as online applications.

Protecting Your Supply Chain

Many aspects of the IP theft problem are in the hands of government and law enforcement officials and beyond the control of businesses. But one important area over which businesses can exert a large measure of control is the security of their supply chain. Lax security creates opportunities for counterfeit and stolen goods to make their way into legitimate production, wholesale, and retail channels.

To assist businesses and raise awareness of the importance of supply chain security, the U.S. Chamber of Commerce, through its Coalition Against Counterfeiting and Piracy, has developed a toolkit of best practices, which companies in a variety of industry sectors are using to improve their internal systems. To access the toolkit, go to http://www.thetruecosts.org/portal/truecosts/resources/supplychain.

Protecting Your IPR at Trade Shows

Products on display at trade shows may be susceptible to IP theft. Most people attend trade shows to market their products, learn the latest industry trends, and check out the competition. Unfortunately, IP thieves have been attending trade shows and surfing the Internet in increasing numbers in order to rip off legitimate businesses. It is essential, therefore, that you take steps to protect all IPRs in your products before displaying those products at trade shows.

In addition to being sites where IP is stolen, trade shows are also places where IP thieves display their infringing products. As a result, they are excellent venues for monitoring infringement of your IP. Before attending a trade show, you should determine in advance what IP policies and procedures are in place and what you will need to combat IP theft (e.g., proof of ownership of patents/trademarks/copyrights, lawyers on call to quickly obtain a court order or contact law enforcement officials). Note that many trade shows have policies that preclude the organizers from mediating disputes that may arise in connection with the show. They will respond, however, to court orders and instructions from law enforcement officials. If the U.S. Commercial Service is present at the trade show, you also can contact them for information on how to resolve an IP dispute. You may be advised to contact a local lawyer who can help you take the legal steps necessary to stop the infringement.

Module 5: Obtaining and Protecting Your IPRs Abroad

Lesson 1: How to Obtain and Protect Your IPRs Abroad

Introduction

For many businesses, protection of intellectual property rights (IPRs) in the United States is only the first step. If your business conducts any of its activities abroad, or if there is any possibility that it may do so in the future, you must take steps to protect your intellectual property (IP) assets in foreign markets.

Increasingly, even those businesses that consider themselves "U.S. only" need to take steps to protect their IP assets outside the United States in order, for example, to protect the IPRs in their Web sites and to protect themselves against imports of counterfeit and pirated goods from other countries.

Overview of IPR Protection in Foreign Markets

Efforts to protect IP in foreign markets generally focus on trademarks and patents, rather than copyright, because trademarks and patents are territorial. Copyright protection generally does not depend upon procedures or formalities in individual countries; the mere creation of a copyrightable work is generally sufficient for copyright protection to exist in many countries of the world. In contrast, protection of trademarks and patents in foreign countries requires that affirmative steps to secure rights be taken in each country where protection is desired. Accordingly, this module focuses upon steps necessary to protect trademarks and patents abroad.

Navigating the procedural requirements in foreign countries can be difficult, and the assistance of an attorney in the country where registration is desired is generally necessary. In most cases, U.S. IP attorneys will work directly with foreign counsel to secure the necessary registrations.

To better inform yourself about protecting IP in foreign markets, you may look up the Web sites for IP authorities in different countries at www.wipo.int/members/en. You may also access information on the IP protection schemes in different countries through various IP "toolkits" provided at www.stopfakes.gov.

Deciding Where to Obtain IPR Protection

Protecting IPRs in every corner of the globe, while ideal, is generally impractical for all but a handful of the largest corporations. Decisions need to be made, therefore, regarding where IPR protection can and should be pursued. Factors to consider when deciding where to seek IPR protection include the:

- Locations of current and future markets for products and/or services

- Locations for current and future ancillary business operations

In addition to protecting IPRs in countries where products or services are likely to be sold, a business should also consider obtaining IPR protection in countries where it has (or may have in the future) ancillary business operations, such as:
   o The purchase of parts or supplies
   o The manufacture of products or product parts
   o Research and development
   o Customer services call centers
   o Distribution centers
   o Transshipment of goods/services

- Benefits and costs of protection in particular countries

In addition to the benefit of protecting against infringement, securing registrations in foreign countries, particularly of patents and trademarks, provides additional benefits to a business. Some of these benefits may include:
   o Increasing the company's value and visibility
   o Making the company more attractive to investors
   o Helping to secure financing
   o Allowing the company to demand higher prices
   o Increasing revenue through licensing

Businesses should carefully evaluate potential benefits in order to assess whether the benefits will outweigh the costs of obtaining foreign patents or trademark registration. For many small businesses, the benefits of foreign IPR protection, particularly patents, may not exceed costs.

- Degree of infringement activity and enforcement in particular countries

Other important factors in deciding where to obtain IPR protection abroad are the amount of infringement activity in a particular country and the adequacy and effectiveness of enforcement mechanisms to address infringement. Keep in mind, however, that there are some countries with weak enforcement systems where seeking protection of IPRs may nevertheless be advisable.

One way business owners can evaluate how effective IP enforcement is in individual countries is to review the United States Trade Representative (USTR) Annual Special 301 Report, which examines the adequacy and effectiveness of IPR enforcement in various countries. The most current USTR Special 301 Report can be found at http://www.ustr.gov.

- Nature of the business and IPR to be protected

    Laws differ in various countries regarding the scope of protection for certain types of trademarks and patents. For example, some countries protect sounds as trademarks, while others do not. In addition, some countries allow patents to be issued for computer software, while others do not.

    Similarly, market conditions may be favorable for products in some countries but not in others due to trade barriers that different countries have erected.

    A good resource to evaluate the market conditions for particular products and services is the National Trade Estimate Report on Foreign Trade Barriers, which can be found at: www.ustr.gov.

Deciding When to Seek IPR Protection in Foreign Markets

Companies should consider obtaining IPR rights in foreign markets as quickly as possible. In foreign markets where a business is already operating or into which the business reasonably expects to expand, IPR protection should be established simultaneously with, or quickly following, efforts to establish IPR protection in the United States. The urgency of seeking foreign IP protection arises from the laws of various countries pertaining to trademarks and patents.

With regard to trademarks, most countries in the world (other than the United States, the United Kingdom, Canada, and a few others) have "first to file" systems. In "first to file" countries, trademark rights are granted to the first party to register a mark in the country, regardless of who may have used the mark first in that country. Therefore, a U.S. business that has established significant brand recognition in its trademark may find itself unable to use that brand name in a foreign market if another party has beaten it to registration.

Similarly, inventors must keep in mind that most countries have "first to file" patent systems, which means that patents are granted to the first party to seek a patent rather than the first party to invent the patentable subject matter. In addition, most countries other than the United States bar an inventor from obtaining a patent if the invention is publicly disclosed before a patent application is filed.

Establishing Trademark Rights Abroad

Anyone seeking to establish trademark rights in other countries should:

- Conduct trademark searches in those countries.

    Searches always should be conducted before selecting a new trademark to determine whether the proposed mark would be likely to cause confusion in the marketplace with another mark already registered or in use. An Internet search is a good first step to get a general sense of how a proposed mark is being used around the world. Some trademark offices provide access to their trademark search databases on their Web sites, but professional trademark searches should also be conducted to ensure that use of the mark will not infringe the rights of any prior user or registrant.

If a mark has already been in use in the United States and the business is now expanding to foreign markets, new searches should be conducted for marks registered and in use in the countries into which the business seeks to expand.

U.S. businesses or individuals seeking to conduct trademark searches should contact an experienced trademark attorney to assist with this process.

- File applications to register the trademark in each country where trademark protection is desired. When applying for trademark registrations, applicants should consider:

  o *Filing in "first to use" countries*
     Trademark registration is not required to establish trademark rights in countries with "first to use" trademark systems, such as the United States. Nevertheless, trademark registration in those countries confers considerable benefits on the trademark owner, and registration in those countries should be seriously considered.

     In countries with "first to file" trademark protection systems, registration is necessary to protect a mark, and registration in those countries, if desired, should be pursued as quickly as possible.

  o *Taking advantage of international filing systems, such as:*
     - Madrid Protocol
        The Protocol Relating to the Madrid Agreement Concerning the International Registration of Marks (Madrid Protocol) is an international treaty that allows a trademark owner to seek registration in any of the countries that are parties to it by filing an international application. The International Bureau of the World Intellectual Property Organization (WIPO), in Geneva, administers the international registration system.

        U.S. trademark owners seeking to file in some or all of the Madrid Protocol member countries may file an international application with the U.S. Patent and Trademark Office (USPTO). If the necessary filing requirements are met, the USPTO will forward the Madrid Protocol application to the International Bureau of WIPO in Geneva. The principal benefits of the Madrid Protocol filing system are convenience and cost savings. Rather than filing individual applications in each member country, the Madrid

Protocol allows applicants to file a single application for registration in dozens of countries for a single filing fee. More than 70 countries, including the United States and the European Union (EU), are members of the Madrid Protocol. For more information on the Madrid Protocol, go to: www.uspto.gov/web/trademarks/madrid/madridindex.htm.

- ▪ Community Trade Mark (CTM)
  The CTM offers the opportunity to protect a trademark in all of the countries of the EU by filing a single application. Applications for a CTM may be made either directly at the Office for Harmonization in the Internal Market in Alicante Spain, or at the trademark office of any of the EU member states.

  Note that because the EU is a member of the Madrid Protocol, it is not necessary for a trademark owner to file both Madrid Protocol and CTM applications. However, if registration is sought only in the EU and not in all of the other Madrid Protocol countries, a CTM application may be a more efficient and less costly alternative. For more information on the Madrid Protocol versus the CTM, see: www.inta.org/index.php?option=com_content&task=view&id=192 &Itemid=132&getcontent=1.

- o *Claiming Paris Convention priority*
  According to the Paris Convention (Stockholm Act 1967), if a trademark application is filed in the applicant's country of origin and the same application is filed in other signatory countries within 6 months after the first application was filed, the applicant can claim the filing date of the first application in the country of origin in the later filed applications. This filing date is the priority date for purposes of establishing rights in the Paris Convention members' territories.

- o *Filing for both phonetic and conceptual translations of marks*
  When registering trademarks in a foreign country, it may be advisable to translate the mark into the country's native language. In countries that do not use roman characters in their native language, such as countries in Asia and the Middle East, you may wish to consider registering: (a) the English version of the mark; (b) the phonetic translation (transliteration) of the mark (e.g., SONY can be transliterated in Chinese as suo ni, which means "'cable" (suo) and "nun" (ni); and (c) a conceptual equivalent of the mark (e.g., the trademark SHELL could be translated into the Chinese bei ke, which means "shell"). In some cases, the best approach may be to combine the conceptual and phonetic methods. For example, COCA-COLA in Chinese consists of the Chinese characters pronounced ke kou

ke le, which has a sound close to the original pronunciation and means "tasty and happiness producing."

The following is an example of a hypothetical business and the steps it would need to take to protect its trademark rights abroad:

Nifty Products, Inc. (NPI), a U.S. company, has created a revolutionary new coffeemaker. The coffeepot will be sold under the name "WonderPot." Prior to its U.S. product launch, NPI files an intent-to-use application to register the WONDERPOT mark with the U.S. Patent and Trademark Office (USPTO).

NPI anticipates that its coffeepot will be a major success, and although it plans to launch the product in the United States, it has hopes of expanding sales to overseas markets within 2 years. Therefore, a month after getting its U.S. trademark application on file, NPI's attorneys assist NPI with trademark searches for the WONDERPOT name in other countries into which NPI plans to expand, including Australia, Korea, Japan, China, and each of the EU countries. Those searches do not reveal any conflict with the WONDERPOT name, and NPI instructs its attorneys to file trademark applications for WONDERPOT in all the countries searched. NPI would like to delay the expenditures associated with foreign trademark applications, but NPI's attorneys advise NPI that it can claim an earlier priority date under the Paris Convention if it gets those foreign applications on file within 6 months of the U.S. application. Based upon that advice, NPI instructs its attorneys to proceed.

NPI's attorneys give NPI the good news that it needs to file only a single application in order to secure trademark registrations in all of the countries in which it seeks trademark protection. This application can be filed using the Madrid Protocol because all of the countries in which NPI seeks protection are members of that international agreement. Equally good news is that NPI's Madrid Protocol application can be filed through the USPTO.

NPI makes sure that all of its products bear proper trademark notices. NPI is now in a strong position to protect its trademark rights at home and abroad.

Maintaining Trademark Rights Abroad

Once trademark rights have been established in foreign countries, steps must be taken to ensure that those rights are properly maintained. As in the United States, failure to take appropriate steps to maintain a trademark in a foreign country can result in abandonment of the trademark rights. Steps that should be taken to ensure that trademark rights are properly maintained in foreign countries include:

– Continuous use of the mark

As in the United States, trademarks rights must be maintained through actual use of the trademark. Most countries have provisions for cancellation of a trademark registration in the event of nonuse for a certain period of time, which is usually a period of either 3 or 5 years. If the mark is not used for the prescribed period of time, a court may find the mark to have been abandoned, thereby enabling others to use the mark.

- Consistent and proper use of the mark

  It is customary in the United States to use the symbols TM (trademark) and SM (service mark) in connection with marks that are not registered and the symbol ® in connection with marks that are registered. While trademark symbols are customarily used in the United States, not all countries recognize them. Therefore, when using the marks in connection with products or advertisements that may be distributed outside of the United States, use a trademark attribution notice such as "[TRADEMARK] is a trademark of [Owner], registered in the U.S. and other countries."

- Enforcement of rights in the mark

  As trademark owner must take action against third parties who, without the trademark owner's consent, use a mark that is confusingly similar to their mark. Failure to police infringers can progressively weaken the mark's image and strength and may, over time, cause the mark to be declared abandoned.

- Making necessary filings to maintain registrations

  As with U.S. trademark registrations, periodic filings and fees are required to maintain foreign trademark registrations. The rules in each country are different, and trademark owners should enlist the aid of local trademark attorneys to assist with maintenance of foreign registrations.

- Proper licensing contracts and oversight

  All trademark licensing agreements should be in writing, and trademark owners must exercise quality control oversight over all products and services offered to the consumer by a licensee under the owner's mark.

Establishing Patent Rights Abroad

Anyone seeking to obtain patent rights in other countries should:

- Conduct patent searches in those countries to determine whether the invention is patentable and whether the invention is already covered by another patent in that country.
- File applications to register the patent in each country where patent protection is desired. Patent applications vary by country, but like the United States, patent applications generally must include:

- A description of the invention, usually accompanied by drawings, plans, or diagrams
- Specific claims that indicate the scope of protection being sought in the patent

When applying for patents in foreign countries, applicants should consider:

- "First to invent" vs. "first to file" countries

  The United States has a "first to invent" system, which means that a patent will be granted to the person or persons shown to be the first inventor of the subject matter in question. This system differs from almost all other countries, which have a "first to file" system that awards the patent to the first to file a patent application regardless of who invented it first. Patent applications in "first to file" countries should be pursued as soon as possible to avoid losing patent rights to others who file first.

- Rules with regard to public disclosure in foreign countries (risk of losing patent rights)

  U.S. law allows a 1-year grace period after public disclosure or certain uses or sales of an invention in which to file a U.S. patent application. In contrast, most other countries bar an inventor from obtaining a patent if the invention is publicly disclosed before a patent application is filed. Therefore, in order to preserve patent rights in foreign countries, U.S. inventors should be cautious in deciding when to disclose inventions and when to file applications abroad.

- International agreements that aid in patent protection internationally, including:

  - *Paris Convention*
    The Paris Convention helps inventors from signatory countries seeking to establish rights in other countries by granting them the right to claim an earlier filing date in subsequent patent applications. Specifically, if an inventor files patent applications in other signatory countries within 1 year of filing his or her original application (usually in his or her home country), the later applications will carry the filing date of the first application.
  - *Patent Cooperation Treaty (PCT)*
    The PCT provides for the filing of a single international patent application that has the same effect as filing individual applications in the countries that are members of the PCT. The PCT provides for a two-step examination procedure:

    1. The patent office receiving an application makes a preliminary examination of the application.

2. National patent offices in PCT member countries review the application, giving weight to the conclusions reached in the preliminary examination.

Note that after the filing of the initial application, the application will be examined separately by each PCT member country, and separate fees will need to be paid to each country examining the application.

The PCT has more than 135 members, including the United States and most developed nations of the world. A current list of PCT members can be found at: http://www.wipo.int/pct/guide/en/gdvol1/annexes/annexa/ax_a.pdf.

U.S. inventors should file their PCT applications with a special branch of the USPTO called the U.S. Receiving Office. For information and assistance regarding the PCT application process, go to: http://www.uspto.gov/web/offices/pac/dapp/pctlegaladminmain.html.

For more information about establishing patent rights abroad, including estimates of costs associated with that process, see the General Accountability Office (GAO) report entitled "Experts' Advice for Small Businesses Seeking Foreign Patents" posted at www.stopfakes.gov.

The following is an example of a hypothetical company and the lessons it learned about protecting patents abroad:

Biotech Corporation (Biotech) is a small pharmaceuticals company based in California. In July 2001, Biotech completed work on a promising new drug for treating heart attack victims. In January 2002, Biotech filed for a U.S. patent covering the composition of the drug, which was granted in March 2003.

In December 2003, Biotech filed a patent application for the drug in Japan. In March 2004, Japan's Patent Office issued a notice to Biotech advising that it had rejected Biotech's patent application because of lack of novelty, citing a prior pending patent application filed in February 2003 by Advanced Medical Ltd. (AML), a U.K. pharmaceuticals company. AML had simultaneously been developing a drug that was almost identical to Biotech's drug, and AML had completed work on its drug in December 2002.

Biotech is furious that its patent application has been rejected in Japan, and it has pointed out to all concerned that it invented the drug before AML. Further, Biotech argues that it filed the Japan patent application well within 1 year from the date that its U.S. patent was granted and that its Japan patent application should therefore have been given priority status.

Unfortunately for Biotech, it is in a very weak position to challenge AML's Japanese patent because it did not take appropriate steps to protect its rights. The fact that Biotech invented its drug first is irrelevant to the question of priority in Japan because Japan is a "first to file" country, rather than a "first to invent" country. Biotech could have secured a prior filing date pursuant to the Paris Convention, but it appears to have misunderstood the requirements for doing so.

Under the Paris Convention, if an inventor files a foreign patent application within 1 year of filing his or her original application (usually in his or her home country), the later application will carry the filing date of the first application. In this case, Biotech filed its Japan patent application within 1 year of its U.S. patent being granted, rather than 1 year after the filing of its U.S patent application. Therefore, it was too late to claim Paris Convention priority.

It should also be noted that Biotech should have considered filing a PCT application rather than seeking protection only in Japan. If it had done so, it could have secured priority in many foreign countries through a single filing.

Maintaining Patent Rights Abroad

Once patent rights have been established in foreign countries, the following steps must be taken to ensure that those rights are properly maintained. Failure to properly maintain a patent may result in those rights being compromised or abandoned.

- Renewal or maintenance fees

    Typically, in order to maintain patent rights for the full term of protection, fees must be paid on a regular basis in each country where a patent has been granted. If the fees are not paid, the patent will cease to remain in force and the invention will fall into the public domain. These fees are typically referred to as "renewal" or "maintenance" fees. In countries where maintenance fees are paid annually, they are sometimes called annuities.

    Each country has its own rules regarding the timing of required maintenance fees. It is advisable, if possible, to retain the services of an attorney to ensure that patent maintenance fees are paid on time. There are also companies which specialize in worldwide patent maintenance programs.

    Note that, unlike trademarks, patents cannot be renewed beyond the established term of protection (typically 20 years). Although some countries refer to the required fees as "renewal" fees, the purpose of those fees is to maintain the patent for the full term of protection, rather than to seek additional time beyond that term.

    You pay maintenance fees to prevent your patent rights from expiring before the maximum 20 years. The date upon which your maintenance fee becomes due depends on the filing date of your patent. The first payment is due no later than the 2nd anniversary of the filing of your application and on each subsequent anniversary of the date of filing, up to the 19th year.

- Patent "working" requirements

The concept of "working" a patented invention was designed to ensure that the public in the country granting the patent benefited from it. For example, if Country X granted a patent for widgets but the patent owner did not manufacture widgets in Country X, the patent owner will have failed to "work" the patent in that country. In that event, Country X might issue a license to anyone who was willing to manufacture the widgets in Country X and to provide reasonable compensation to the patent owner for that license.

An international agreement pertaining to patents states that "patents shall be available and patent rights enjoyable without discrimination as to . . . whether products are imported or locally produced." The U.S. position is that this provision prohibits other countries (who are signatories to the agreement) from requiring a patent owner to manufacture a patented invention in that country. Rather, importation of the patented invention into a country must be allowed to satisfy working requirements.

Some countries, however, maintain that they have a right to require that a patented invention be manufactured in their country. If there is no manufacture within a prescribed time period, the patent may be void or subject to the grant of a "compulsory license" to any person who may apply for a license (i.e., the government of that country grants a third party the right to manufacture the patented invention without the consent of the patent holder).

- Enforcement of patent against infringement

The exclusive rights granted to a patent holder are meaningless if steps are not taken to enforce the patent against infringement. The more successful an invention is on the commercial market, the more likely it is that these rights will be infringed.

Unfortunately, enforcement of patent rights is extremely expensive; consequently, effective patent enforcement can be a substantial challenge for small-to-medium sized businesses or lone inventors.

Other Steps to Protect IPRs Abroad

In addition to the other measures discussed in this lesson for protecting IPRs in foreign countries, there are three additional steps that business owners can take to ensure the value in their IP is protected. These steps include:

– Conducting due diligence on overseas business partners

Before entering into business relationships with overseas enterprises and even prior to entering into discussions or potential business arrangements, it is essential to conduct thorough due diligence on the prospective business partner to ensure it does not have a history of criminal behavior, IP theft, or other behavior that could be a threat to your business.

The U.S. Commercial Service helps U.S. companies evaluate potential foreign partners. To contact Commercial Service offices in countries around the world, go to: http://www.buyusa.gov/home/worldwide_us.html.

– Including IPR provisions in licensing contracts and subcontracts

A significant part of the economic value of IP comes from its use in licensing. A well-drafted, written contract is an essential component of any licensing agreement. A poorly drafted contract can result in IPRs being inadvertently lost or compromised.

In most countries, contracts need not be long or even overly formal, but they must be clear and contain the correct language concerning IPRs. Also, each country may have different contracting requirements and procedures, so a "one-size" contract does not necessarily fit all. It is important to get expert legal advice in this area.

– Hiring a service to monitor the market

In some markets, it is possible to hire a service to monitor the market and collect information on counterfeit operations in the marketplace. As with any business partner, conduct due diligence when selecting a service. For example:

- o Interview the service provider and ask critical questions on the depth of their experience and capacity to meet your goals. Inquire as to the manpower with deep cover and surveillance experience, advanced technology equipment and evidence collection experience.
- o Seek references from previous clients and be careful of companies that promise to deliver 100 percent results.
- o Explain your company's goals related to identifying possible infringers.
- o Educate the service provider about your production methods, distribution channels, and pricing.
- o Manage the service provider's work as you would an internal division of your company. Check their work by requesting original documentation, photos, and video. Confirm results when possible with enforcement agencies.

Module 6: Enforcing Your IPRs

Lesson 1: How to Enforce Your IPRs

Introduction

Because intellectual property rights (IPRs) are private rights, it is the responsibility of the right holder to protect them. However, governmental authorities also play a role in ensuring that the infringing activity is stopped and that piracy and counterfeiting on a commercial scale are effectively deterred.

Monitoring the Market for IPR Infringement

In order to stop infringements that could damage your business's reputation and undermine the value of your IPRs, you must actively monitor the marketplace for unauthorized uses of your trademarks, copyrights, or patents. Examples of monitoring activities include:

- Putting in place your own program or hiring a service that monitors the market for infringement through techniques such as conducting wholesale, retail, and Internet buys; technical and physical surveillance; undercover operations; and market analyses
- Hiring a trademark watch service to monitor official publications showing applications or registrations for trademarks in various countries in the world

If you become aware of any infringements of your IPRs, you should confer with your attorney about whether to communicate your rights to the infringer and, if necessary, defend your rights through legal action. The remainder of this module provides information about legal remedies and procedures available to address infringements of IPRs.

Border Enforcement by U.S. Customs and Border Protection

CBP has established border enforcement procedures to prevent the entry of infringing goods into domestic commerce. Recording federally-registered trademarks and copyrights with CBP is simple and can be done regardless of whether you suspect infringing goods are entering the United States. Recordation can be done online by logging on to the CBP website's IPR Recordation page at https://apps.cbp.gov/e-recordations.

At the time of recordation or anytime after recordation, you can also alert CBP if you suspect that a shipment of infringing goods has entered, or might soon enter, the United States. In this case, you should send an email about the allegation. The email should:

- Provide as much information about the alleged infringer, including as much information as possible about the suspect goods, such as:
  - o Possible ports of entry
  - o The name and contact information of the alleged importer, manufacturer, or consignee
  - o The date of arrival of the goods
  - o The vessel on which the goods arrived (or may arrive)
  - o Digital images of both the protected goods and the suspect goods
- Be sent to hqiprbranch@dhs.gov.

The procedures outlined in Module 4 for recording federally-registered trademarks and copyrights with the CBP are similar to the procedures that exist in other countries for enforcing IPRs at the border. You should strongly consider recording your IPRs with customs officials in countries where you do business. Also, unlike the United States, some countries accept recordation of patents. Many countries have information online regarding proper procedures for registering IP with their customs officials. You can get contact information for customs authorities abroad at: http://www.wcoipr.org/wcoipr/Menu_CustomContacts.htm.

Addressing Online Copyright Infringement

Another easy and relatively inexpensive IP enforcement mechanism, known as "notice and takedown," addresses infringement of copyrighted material online. This enforcement mechanism allows a copyright owner to get infringing material taken off a U.S.-owned Web site quickly and easily. The procedure works like this:

- *Step One:* If you come across material on a third-party Web site that infringes your copyright, you can send a letter to the Internet service provider (ISP) that is hosting the Web site (e.g., AOL, Comcast). You must send the letter to the ISP's designated agent and must include certain information and statements required under the law. For a list of ISP designated agents, go to http://www.copyright.gov/onlinesp/list/index.html. Know that a notice to an ISP must include:
  - o The name, address, and electronic signature of the complaining party
  - o An identification of the infringing materials and their Internet location or, if the service provider is an information location tool such as a search engine, the reference or link to the infringing materials
  - o An identification of the copyrighted works that have been infringed
  - o A statement by the copyright owner that it has a good faith belief that the copyrighted material is not being used legally
  - o A statement that the notice is accurate and, under penalty of perjury, that the complaining party is authorized to act on the behalf of the owner
- *Step Two:* If the letter contains all of the required information and statements, the ISP must "take down" (remove or disable access to) the online content in question and must provide notice to the party who posted the content on the Web that it has done so.

- *Step Three:* If the party posting the content feels that it was taken down unfairly, he or she may submit a counter-notice to the ISP ("the put back"). A proper counter-notice must contain the following information:
  - The subscriber's name, address, phone number, and physical or electronic signature
  - Identification of the material removed and its location before removal
  - A statement under penalty of perjury that the material was removed by mistake or misidentification
  - A statement by the subscriber consenting to local Federal court jurisdiction or, if overseas, to any judicial district where the ISP may be found
- *Step Four:* If the ISP receives a proper counter-notice, it must:
  - Notify you that the material will be restored in 10 business days
  - Restore the content between 10 and 14 business days from the date of receipt of the counter- notice, unless the ISP first receives notice from you that you have filed a lawsuit against the party who posted the content on the Web.

Note that any party who misrepresents a claim regarding infringing material could become liable to the ISP for any damages that resulted from the improper removal of the material. Also note that these procedures apply to U.S. disputes; procedures for addressing online infringement by foreign persons or entities may differ, and many countries do not have comparable notice-and-takedown procedures.

Addressing Domain Name Disputes

The explosion of the Internet in the mid-1990s and the race to acquire domain names created some thorny problems for trademark owners around the world. Disputes quickly arose among legitimate trademark owners and between legitimate trademark owners and cybersquatters.

Legitimate trademark owners are businesses and individuals with the legal right to use the same trademark for different products and services often want to use the same domain name. For example, the respective owners of the trademark ROYAL for windows, dill pickles, and financial services all may have wanted to register the domain www.royal.com. On the contrary, Cybersquatters are those who exploit the first-come, first-served nature of the domain name registration system by registering domains incorporating trademarks with which they have no legitimate connection.

In order to facilitate the resolution of domain name disputes around the world, a dispute resolution procedure called the Uniform Domain Name Dispute Resolution Policy (UDRP) was adopted by the Internet Corporation for Assigned Names and Numbers (ICANN). The UDRP is applicable only to disputes over domain names registered in the generic top-level domains (gTLDs) (e.g., .com, .org, .info, .biz). The UDRP was designed to be efficient and cost-effective and has been used to resolve thousands of domain name disputes.

Domain name disputes also arise in country-code top-level domains (ccTLDs). These disputes are handled according to the policies and practices of the specific ccTLD. Some ccTLDs have adopted the UDRP or a modified UDRP, while others have instituted other approaches to resolving disputes. Still others have no system in place for administrative dispute resolution; in those ccTLDs, disputes would be handled through the courts.

A number of organizations have been approved by ICANN to hear and resolve disputes under the UDRP. Information about the UDRP and the approved dispute resolution service providers may be found through the ICANN Web site at www.icann.org/udrp.

Cease and Desist Letters

If border enforcement and online enforcement mechanisms are not sufficient or appropriate to address an IP infringement situation you are facing, you will need to engage the services of an attorney to help you take other steps to confront the problem. Often, the first step to take will be the preparation and delivery of a cease and desist letter. A cease and desist letter is simply a letter that puts the alleged infringer on notice of your rights and asks the alleged infringer to stop the activity that is believed to be infringing.

There are numerous benefits to sending a cease and desist letter as a preliminary step in confronting infringement. Cease and desist letters:

- Frequently facilitate an out-of-court settlement.
    - o Many IP violators are unaware of their violations and are willing to stop their conduct once they receive notice of the problem from the IP owner.
    - o Dialogue with the alleged infringer can help establish facts about the infringement that resolve the matter with only minor changes from the alleged infringer.
- Sometimes enable IP owners to identify the ultimate source of offending merchandise and avoid litigation with parties whose role is merely tangential.
- May put you in a position to recover increased damages in any litigation that may ensue because, by putting the alleged infringer on notice of your rights, continued infringement may be characterized as "willful."

Other Methods of Addressing IP Infringement Without Litigation

If a cease and desist letter does not achieve the desired result, litigation may be necessary to address the infringing activity. There are, however, other steps that an IP owner should consider before resorting to costly and time-consuming litigation. They include:

- Alternative dispute resolution

    There are many reasons why litigation may not be the best method to deal with infringers. IP litigation is complex, and cases often take years to reach a decision. In that time, the IP at issue may become obsolete. In cases involving foreign infringers, jurisdictional issues can be extremely difficult to navigate. Finally, IP litigation is very expensive. For example, in the United States, the total median cost of patent litigation through trial is $1 million.

An alternative to litigation is "alternative dispute resolution (ADR)," a term which refers to dispute resolution methods that do not rely on the traditional court system. One form of ADR that is much less expensive than litigation is mediation. Mediation is a voluntary, non-binding private dispute resolution process in which a neutral person (the mediator) helps the parties try to reach a negotiated settlement. Mediation could be described as a form of assisted settlement conference at which all parties are present and represented by counsel.

Another form of ADR is arbitration, which is binding and final, just like litigation. Although arbitration is more formal than mediation, it is still, in many cases, cheaper and faster than litigation.

The World Intellectual Property Organization (WIPO) Arbitration and Mediation Centre offers ADR services for the resolution of international commercial disputes between private parties. For more information on the WIPO Arbitration and Mediation Centre, go to http://www.wipo.int/amc/en/index.html.

In addition, the International Trademark Association offers ADR in trademark infringement cases. For more information, go to http://www.inta.org/index.php?option=com_content&task=view&id=71&Itemid=219&getcontent=4.

Local bar associations, artist organizations, and industry-specific associations may also offer such services.

– Contact a business association

Industry associations representing the IPR sectors (copyright, trademark, and patent) are very active in the United States and many overseas markets. Representatives from these associations can be excellent resources for "on the ground" perspectives and intelligence. These associations, as well as other industry-specific associations, can also help to assert pressure on foreign governments to take enforcement action against infringers in their countries.

You will find a list of some of the industry associations in the Resource Center.

– Licensing agreements

In some circumstances, demanding a complete halt to infringing activity and compensation for all prior infringing acts may not be the best way to deal with an infringer. A mutually agreeable business resolution, such as offering to license the infringer on commercially reasonable terms, may present a faster, less costly solution to the problem.

Depending upon the circumstances, licensing can enable a company to exploit other markets by allowing the licensee to apply the existing technology to a different market. Licensing to firms for production and distribution to different populations can enable a company to further profit from its technology while protecting itself from the overhead required to participate in foreign markets.

While a license may not make sense in every situation, it is one option that should be considered when determining how to confront an IP infringer.

Overview of Civil and Administrative Proceedings

In some cases, where other methods of enforcement have failed to stop infringing activity, it may be necessary to resort to litigation to address the problem. In such cases, you will need to retain an experienced IP attorney to assist you. The laws and procedures associated with IP litigation are complex, and it is extremely difficult to effectively enforce your legal rights without the assistance of an attorney who specializes in this area of law.

Litigation to address IP infringement takes place before either *civil courts* or *administrative tribunals*.

A *civil court* is a proceeding between two private parties in which one person (the plaintiff) sues another (the defendant) who has caused him or her injury or loss. A judgment in a civil matter does not include the imposition of a criminal sentence. If the plaintiff wins, he or she can receive compensation in the form of damages and/or an order to stop the defendant's infringing activities.

A preliminary injunction is an order that requires a defendant to do or not to do something during the time that a civil case is pending. In the United States, a plaintiff seeking a preliminary injunction has to show he or she will suffer an irreparable injury and that he or she is likely to win the lawsuit. In an IPR infringement case, a preliminary injunction will generally prohibit the alleged infringer from manufacturing or selling the product or service in question while the case is pending. Many trademark cases are settled with an injunction, i.e., an order to stop selling the infringing goods and to destroy them. Most court cases in the United States are settled or otherwise resolved short of trial.

Administrative tribunals are decision-making bodies that operate within, or in direct relationship with, particular government agencies. Administrative tribunals are not part of a country's judicial court system, although their function is quasi-judicial because it directly affects the legal rights of a person or corporation. Both civil court cases and administrative tribunal cases are considered to be civil proceedings because they do not involve the imposition of criminal penalties.

Countries around the world utilize a myriad of administrative tribunals to address issues relating to IPR. An example of an IPR administrative tribunal in the United States is the Trademark Trial and Appeal Board (TTAB). The TTAB is part of the U.S. Patent and Trademark Office (USPTO), and it hears cases relating to trademark registration, including disputes between conflicting trademark owners relating to trademark applications and registrations.

The decision as to which route is better for you should be made in consultation with your attorney. Both types of proceedings often take a substantial amount of time to reach a conclusion, and while these cases are pending, infringing goods may continue to enter the marketplace or be destroyed. To address this, IP owners can seek provisional measures to immediately stop infringing products from entering the stream of commerce. Provisional measures are legal remedies that are available to put an immediate halt to infringing activity while an infringement case is pending. Examples of provisional measures include:

- *Preliminary injunctions*, which are court orders requiring a defendant to do or not do something during the time that a case is pending. In an IPR case, a preliminary injunction will generally prohibit the alleged infringer from manufacturing or selling the product or service in question while the case is pending
- *Seizure orders*, which are court orders mandating seizure and impoundment of infringing goods at issue at the beginning of a case. Seizure orders can also relate to the infringer's business records.

Again, the availability of such measures in your case should be discussed with your lawyer.

Civil Actions Against Foreign Infringers

If you know the identity of a foreign person or entity shipping infringing products into the United States, and if you meet the necessary legal and jurisdictional requirements, you can file a complaint against the foreign infringer and/or its U.S. importer or distributor in U.S. Federal court. If successful in the litigation, you can recover monetary damages and obtain an injunction against further infringing activity.

Be aware, however, that civil cases against foreign defendants in U.S. court can be difficult, expensive, and time-consuming. Consult with your attorney about whether this option is appropriate.

Administrative Proceedings Against Foreign Infringers

In recent years, a growing number of IP owners have sought relief from infringing imports by initiating investigations before the United States International Trade

Commission (ITC) under Section 337 of the Tariff Act of 1930. A Section 337 investigation is comparable to the infringement lawsuit an IP owner could file in Federal court, but many IP owners favor proceeding in the ITC because:

- It is easier and faster. There are three primary reasons why a Section 337 investigation typically is faster than an infringement lawsuit filed in Federal court:
  o Section 337 investigations are accelerated proceedings, which means that they are intended to be quicker and more streamlined than court proceedings.
  o Service of process is faster and less expensive in the ITC.
  o Jurisdictional disputes are less common in the ITC because the ITC can take action against the infringing goods and does not need to obtain jurisdiction over the foreign infringer.
- If successful, the IP owner may obtain (1) an exclusion order that prevents infringing products from being imported into the United States, and (2) a "cease and desist order" that bans the sale and distribution of the infringing product within the United States.
- An exclusion order from the ITC relating to a patent right may allow the patent owner to obtain customs enforcement of patent rights that are not available simply by recording a patent with the CBP. (While the CBP does not have legal authority to determine patent infringement on its own, it can enforce exclusion orders obtained from the ITC.)

Although a Section 337 proceeding is generally faster than a civil court case, it is nevertheless very expensive, as it requires significant time and effort by an attorney to navigate to final resolution. Also note that an IP owner must have a registered patent, trademark or copyright to initiate a Section 337 proceeding. Further information pertaining to Section 337 investigations can be found at http://www.usitc.gov/trade_remedy/int_prop/index.htm.

Criminal Proceedings

Because profits from the sale of counterfeit and pirated goods are so enormous, monetary damages, administrative fines, and seizures and destruction of infringing goods are not always effective in deterring this activity. Accordingly, criminal proceedings are sometimes necessary, particularly in cases of trademark counterfeiting and copyright piracy that are willful and on a commercial scale.

Criminal penalties include:

- Imprisonment and/or monetary fines
- Seizure and destruction of infringing goods and equipment used in their manufacture
-

If you have knowledge of IP theft, contact the National IPR Center through http://www.ice.gov/pi/cornerstone/ipr/index.htm.

Summary

You have now completed the Understanding Intellectual Property Rights course.